Sustainability in the Hospitality Industry

Sustainability in the Hospitality Industry
Principles of Sustainable Operations

Philip Sloan
Department of Hospitality Management
International University of Applied Sciences Bad Honnef – Bonn,
Bad Honnef, Germany

Willy Legrand
Department of Hospitality Management
International University of Applied Sciences Bad Honnef – Bonn,
Bad Honnef, Germany

Joseph S. Chen
Department of Recreation, Park and Tourism Studies
Indiana University, Bloomington, USA

ELSEVIER

AMSTERDAM • BOSTON • HEIDELBERG • LONDON • NEW YORK • OXFORD
PARIS • SAN DIEGO • SAN FRANCISCO • SINGAPORE • SYDNEY • TOKYO
Butterworth-Heinemann is an imprint of Elsevier

Butterworth-Heinemann is an imprint of Elsevier
Linacre House, Jordan Hill, Oxford OX2 8DP, UK
30 Corporate Drive, Suite 400, Burlington, MA 01803, USA

First edition 2009

British Library Cataloguing-in-Publication Data
A catalogue record for this book is available from the British Library

Library of Congress Cataloging-in-Publication Data
A catalog record for this book is available from the Library of Congress

ISBN: 978-0-7506-7968-8

For information on all Butterworth–Heinemann
publications visit our Web site at www.elsevierdirect.com

Typeset by Macmillan Publishing Solutions
(www.macmillansolutions.com)

Printed and bound in Great Britain

09 10 11 12   10 9 8 7 6 5 4 3 2 1

Contents

Preface

The hoteliers' relationship toward environmental challenges and societal concerns is one of a rather remote and intangible nature met with varying levels of interests. However, these concerns have been high on the public agenda for the past few years following substantial press coverage of environmental degradation and the polarization of modern society. Shareholders, employees and customers all have higher expectations of a Hospitality Industry that increasingly demonstrates responsible behavior across the triple bottom line of economic, social and environmental management. In response, the Hospitality Industry along with governments and private organizations are launching initiatives that help hoteliers become more sustainable, i.e. by becoming more environmentally responsible and by working in harmony with society at large.

A clear understanding of the issues surrounding climate change, global warming, air and water pollution, ozone depletion, deforestation, the loss of biodiversity and global poverty is essential for successful implementation of sustainable business management strategies.

This book is of particular interest for three reasons.

Firstly, there is acute pressure on all in the private sector to reduce environmental impacts and clean up after themselves. All stakeholders including investors, employees, customers, environmental and ethical groups as well as the general public expect companies to demonstrate best practice in all dimensions of the 'triple bottom line', i.e. social well-being, environmental stewardship and healthy economic performance. Companies are increasingly judged by their adherence to these principles and their transparency on how they communicate actions and results. Although the hospitality sector does not count amongst the great polluters such as the metallurgical or chemical industries, the size and rapid growth of the industry makes it clear that environmentally sustainable action is necessary. This book analyzes trends in environmental protection and social equity and reviews best hospitality industry practices regarding reduced water and energy consumption, green design and the sourcing of sustainable fixtures, fittings and food and beverage products.

Secondly, environmental legislation is becoming more stringent and complex, with stricter emission and pollution controls than ever before. The tourism industry, as a whole, is one of the largest industries of the world, responsible for 10.3% of global GDP and 234 million jobs worldwide corresponding to 8.7% of total employment (WTO, 2008). For businesses, the challenge is to be a step ahead of legislation by adopting preventative strategies rather than 'end of pipe' or cleanup practices. This book examines how hotels and restaurants can implement environmental management systems, and how business competitive advantages can be gained through certification and eco-labeling procedures.

Thirdly, by incorporating responsible marketing and corporate social responsibility policies, hospitality businesses can enhance their reputation and attract investment. This book examines the behavior of the responsible consumer and the sustainable marketing practices considered necessary to attract such consumers.

Sustainability in the Hospitality Industry seeks to provide answers to these questions by producing inventive solutions to contemporary environmental, social and economical challenges. This book is designed to provide guidance to students and hospitality professionals wishing to develop a clear understanding of a new sustainable business parameter that will hopefully be of benefit to present and future generations alike.

Acknowledgment

We would like to first thank our families and friends who relentlessly encouraged our endeavor and share the effort by supporting the book project.

We are also grateful to our affiliations, the International University of Applied Sciences Bad Honnef – Bonn and the Department of Recreation, Park and Tourism Studies at Indiana University, which have made our research efforts concerning sustainable hospitality management possible. We owe special thanks to many colleagues for providing us with intellectual guidance and inspiration.

Thank you to hotels and restaurants which constantly thrive to improve business in a sustainable manner, providing this book with valuable material.

Finally, our sincere thanks to the hospitality students of the International University of Applied Sciences Bad Honnef – Bonn who have over the years provided valuable support in terms of research, ideas and discussion for this book.

About the Authors

Philip Sloan
Department of Hospitality Management
International University of Applied Sciences Bad Honnef – Bonn

Philip Sloan is one of the founding members of the lecturing team that started at the International University of Applied Sciences Bad Honnef – Bonn in September 2000. After completing hotel school at Portsmouth University in England, Philip held Marketing and General Management positions in London hotels before opening his own specialty restaurants in the UK and later in France. During the next few years, he went on to obtain a master's degree in Environmental Management and an MBA while simultaneously working as an educational consultant on several projects in the Baltic countries at the Council of Europe. In addition to teaching hospitality management studies, Philip works as a consultant giving seminars on sustainable business practices to the Hospitality Industry. He has also recently published articles in scientific journals such as the *International Journal of Hospitality Management*, *Tourism Review International*, *Advances in Hospitality and Leisure* and *Tourism: An interdisciplinary journal*. Keen organic gardeners Philip Sloan with co-author Willy Legrand created an organic vineyard at the International University of Applied Sciences Bad Honnef – Bonn in spring 2008 as an educational project for hospitality management students.

Willy Legrand
Department of Hospitality Management
International University of Applied Sciences Bad Honnef – Bonn

Willy Legrand is lecturing in the Department of Hospitality Management at the International University of Applied Sciences Bad Honnef – Bonn, Germany. After completing his undergraduate degree in Geography, Willy held numerous managerial positions in the hospitality industry in Canada and Germany, before accepting a position at the International University of Applied Sciences Bad Honnef – Bonn in the spring of 2003. Willy holds a master of Business Administration degree with a specialization in Environmental Management. In Bad Honnef, he teaches a variety of courses within the Hospitality curriculum. As a guest lecturer, Willy teaches under-graduate courses on Sustainability in Hospitality Management in various international universities. His recent publications include articles in journals such as *International Journal of Hospitality Management*, *Journal of Culinary Science and Technology*, *Florida International University Hospitality Review*, *Tourism Review International and Advances in Hospitality and Leisure* and *Tourism: An interdisciplinary Journal*. Willy's personal background includes formative years spent working in agriculture and a family involved in organic cultivation and production. As a wine enthusiast and founder of the university's wine club, Willy, together with co-author Philip Sloan, created an organic vineyard, which functions as an educational tool for hospitality management students.

Joseph S. Chen

Department of Recreation, Park and Tourism Studies
Indiana University at Bloomington

Prof. Joseph Chen, a tenured faculty member from the Department of Recreation, Park and Tourism Studies at Indiana University at Bloomington, USA, received his PhD from Pennsylvania State University, USA. Prior to his academic career, Dr. Chen had worked in the hotel and restaurant business in California, USA. His research areas entail consumer behaviors, healthy food choice and health tourism. Consequently, he has produced over 120 scholarly works in refereed journals, conference proceedings and book chapters. Many of this research works appeared in the top-tier research journals. In 2007 he was regarded as one of the top-50 leading tourism scholars between 1985 and 2004 by a peer-reviewed article from *Tourism Management* – A SSCI refereed journal. In addition, in 2008, he was also identified as one of the top-50 most cited tourism scholars between 1998 and 2007 by a peer-reviewed article from *Tourism Management*. He has received international research awards and fellowships including US Fulbright Senior Scholar. Concerning his service to tourism academia, he is the founding editor and the editor-in-chief of *Advances in Hospitality and Leisure* that is a refereed journal published by Emerald, UK. Further, he is also the co-founder and co-chair of the International Conference on Hospitality and Leisure Applied Research (I-CHLAR) that holds conferences regularly.

CHAPTER 1

Sustainable Development in the Hospitality Industry

Study Objectives

- To explain the way the activities of humankind are affecting the planet
- To describe the various forms of environmental degradation
- To define sustainable development and explain its history
- To explain the three pillars of sustainability
- To give reasons why the hospitality industry needs to become more sustainable
- To give examples of sustainable practice in the hospitality industry
- To explain the concept of eco-advantage

CONTENTS

EMERGING CHALLENGES ON THE PLANET

Introduction

Human activities have influenced the earth's ecosystem for many thousands of years. Nowadays the negative consequences of human actions can be noticed everywhere. Being one of the larger industries in the world, the hospitality industry is an important contributor to these problems. In this chapter, it is explained why hospitality operations need to manage their environmental impacts and exactly what is involved in running a profitable business in line with the principles of environmental stewardship and to the benefit of society, i.e. sustainable hospitality management.

1

Problem definition

Travel and tourism is one of the largest industries of the world, responsible for US$6.5 trillion in economic activity, 10.3% of global GDP and 234 million jobs worldwide in 2006, which corresponds to 8.7% of total employment according to the World Tourism Organization (WTO, 2006). An industry this big and internationally oriented has an inevitable, large impact on the environment, economies, cultures and societies in general. The hotels, motels and all the various forms of accommodation comprise the largest sector of the travel and tourism industry, and it has been shown that hotels have the highest negative influence on the environment of all commercial buildings. According to estimations, an average hotel releases between 160 and 200 kg of CO_2 per square meter of room floor area per year and water consumption per guest per night is between 170 and 440 l in the average five-star hotel. On average, hotels produce 1 kg of waste per guest per night.

Impact on the planet

Humankind consumes what nature has to offer and in return creates waste and depletes the earth's natural reserves. All our actions have an impact on the earth's ecosystems that are only able to renew themselves at low levels of consumption. For many thousands of years, man's impact on the environment was negligible; however, at the dawn of the industrial revolution all this changed. We now consume more of the earth's resources than the earth can regenerate; hence, the planet is in 'ecological overshoot'. Current consumption levels are simply too high and action needs to be taken as the planet's non-renewable resources are being quickly depleted. This depletion is accelerated by the continuous growth of world population and its changing consumption patterns.

Another consequence of human activity is the changing climate. Climate changes can be observed by measuring the increases in ocean temperatures and global sea levels that result from the melting of the polar ice caps. Scientists expect sea levels to have risen between 10 and 90 cm by 2100. A consensus exists among scientists that the greater part of global warming in the past decades can be attributed to human activities. The existence of the so-called greenhouse gases is vital to the survival of humankind, without them the surface temperature on earth would be approximately 30°C lower. But human activity has caused increases in the concentration of greenhouse gases, which have lead to increases in air temperatures around the globe.

Developing nations of the world lack resources to respond to environmental degradation. For example, in Bangladesh, a 50 cm rise in sea level will place approximately 6 million people at risk from flooding. Climate change can be witnessed in all corners of the earth. Our televisions inform us on at least a weekly basis of the latest episode of flooding and droughts that hit the unfortunate. To summarize, environmental degradation has serious consequences for humankind, and all existing flora and fauna.

As our planet's natural sources become more and more depleted, humankind is urged to become more responsible in their usage of non-renewable resources and look for other renewable resources either in the form of energy, water or raw materials. Governments, consumer groups, non-governmental organizations, e.g. Greenpeace and the World Wide Fund For Nature (WWF), advocate such a 'sustainable' lifestyle.

Defining 'sustainability'

The term 'sustainability' is used from the early 1970s when attention was first drawn to concerns about the environment and overexploitation. The most generally used definition was christened by the World Commission on Environment and Development in 1983. It published a report called *Our Common Future* in 1987. This report became better known as the Brundtland Report, after the commission's chairwoman Gro Harlem Brundtland, former Prime Minister of Norway. The report defines sustainability as 'development that meets the needs of the present without compromising the ability of future generations to meet their own needs'. Building upon this definition, but changing its focus from humankind's responsibility toward future generations to the current balance of the earth's ecological systems, is the definition of sustainable development in the 1991 publication *Caring for the Earth: A Strategy for Sustainable Living* by the United Nations Environment Programme (UNEP) and the WWF: 'improving the quality of human life while living within the carrying capacity of supporting ecosystems'. The addition of economic and socio-cultural aspects to the notion of sustainability came about from the Earth Summit in June 1992, the United Nations Conference on Environment and Development (UNCED) in Agenda 21. Furthermore, this conference focused attention on the role of education, more specifically education that encourages values and attitudes of respect for the environment. In 2002, the Johannesburg Summit broadened the definition of sustainable development even further by including the notions of social justice and the fight against poverty. Additionally, to reinforce the focus on sustainability and education following a proposal from the Johannesburg Summit in 2002, the United Nations General Assembly proclaimed the period 2005–2014 to be the 'Decade of Education for Sustainable Development'.

Other definitions of sustainability

World Business Council on Sustainable Development

> *We define sustainable developments as forms of progress that meet the needs of the present without compromising the ability of future generations to meet their needs. Given the scale of poverty today, the challenge of meeting present needs is urgent. Given the damage our past and present actions may visit upon our descendants, concern for future needs for environmental, human, social, and other resources is also compelling.*

> *WBCSD (2002)*

World Tourism Organization

> *Sustainability principles refer to the environmental, economic and sociocultural aspects of tourism development, and a suitable balance must be established between these three dimensions to guarantee its long-term sustainability.*

> *(©UNWTO, 9284401109)*

Defining a sustainable hospitality operation

Using the Brundtland definition as a starting point, a sustainable hospitality operation can be defined as a hospitality operation that manages its resources in such a way that economic, social and environmental benefits are maximized in order to meet the need of the present generation while protecting and enhancing opportunities for future generations. For greater clarity, this statement requires examination of the following questions:

Which resources used by a hotel impact directly on economic profit, society and the environment?

How can the principles of sustainability be incorporated into a hospitality management system?

What does it mean for a hotel to meet the needs of the present generation while protecting and enhancing opportunities for future generations?

Sustainable hospitality operations or 'green hotels' aim at reducing their impact on the environment and society. The American association, Green Hotels, provides a more resource-oriented definition: 'green hotels are environmentally sustainable properties whose managers are eager to institute programs that save water, save energy and reduce solid waste while saving money to help protect our one and only earth'.

Critics of sustainability

Although interest and support for sustainable development is growing continuously, critics of the movement and skeptics exist as well. Since numerous definitions of the term 'sustainability' have been created and received media coverage it is often claimed to be difficult to understand. For some, the concept is vague and fuzzy, and the limited availability of sustainable models is often criticized as well. Sustainability is not a quick panacea for all the ills of the world, although for some it has been thought to be a quick fix.

Impediments to the progress of environmental sustainability

The progress of investments in sustainable hospitality operations is often impeded by misconceptions about what is the bottom line. Many managers and owners of hotels only consider the initial investment costs that are indeed higher when compared to unsustainable solutions. However, the running costs are generally much lower than in those properties that have inefficient equipment. The longer-term return of such investments is most often positive purely in financial terms, even without considering the triple bottom line of environment, society and economics. See also the example provided in Box 1.1.

Box 1.1 Solar Energy in the Hotel Industry

Hawaii's Mauna Lani Bay Hotel had acres of roof space, making it the perfect host for the PV system. The hotel's owners displayed their environmental stripes and saved a substantial sum of money by working with PowerLight Corporation to install a PowerGuard® system of insulating PV roofing tiles. The system covers 10,000 square feet and generates 75 net kilowatts  of electricity. It will reduce the hotel's utility bills enough to pay itself in five years (US Department of Energy, 2006).

Another impediment lies in the internal communication and control within hotel chains. Several hotel corporations already have environmental management programs in place, and some of them are even included in the Dow Jones Sustainability Index. But an important factor determining the effectiveness of these programs is the translation of corporate environmental policies to the individual hotels, i.e. the translation into real actions. Many hotels until now have had problems in articulating in-house or corporate environmental management activities. Most often the manager of a hotel has the freedom to determine the strategies and procedures that seem fit to him. Therefore his attitude toward specific subjects will, for a major part, determine the hotel's actions with respect to that subject when the corporate framework leaves him the room to do so. Furthermore, a difference must be made between company-owned and -managed hotels. Different levels of involvement in franchise agreements exist, all with different levels of imposed procedures. Lesser demanding franchise formulas give the manager more freedom to design his own strategy.

Why should hotels become more sustainable?

Pollution, waste, greenhouse gases and environmental hazards do not necessarily spring to mind when considering the hospitality and tourism industries. Environmental degradation is more readily associated with industries like manufacturing, energy production, steel industry, oil production or the chemical industry. To the onlooker, greening seems much more necessary in industries where the pollution is actually visible. However, while the processes that are necessary in the assembly of service products may be intangible, perishable and consumed as they occur, they often involve the support of a wide spectrum of physical components and reliance on natural resources. Hotels need to reduce their impact on the environment as they count amongst the greatest polluters and resource consumers within the service industries. Major hotel chains that constitute a large percentage of rooms worldwide have a significant potential to decrease their impact on the environment. Moreover, large hotel brands have the financial capacity to invest in technology. Hotel chains also have the opportunity to introduce environmental policies on a corporate strategic level and therefore reduce environmental impact on a large scale. Other service providers, like banks and insurers, are assumed to have less impact on the environment.

Sustainable development in the tourism and hospitality industry

The hospitality industry set about incorporating the philosophy of sustainability in the early 1990s. With the publishing of Agenda 21 for the travel and tourism industry, individual businesses and the hospitality industry were encouraged to adopt codes of conduct, promoting sustainable travel and tourism best practices for the first time. Gradually voluntary guidelines and examples of best practices were established in the industry followed by the introduction of eco-labels and certification procedures. More and more hotels and restaurants are now becoming more sustainable as they embark on a wide range of measures designed to reduce their impact on the environment. Around 80% of European hoteliers are involved in some kind of activity oriented toward the environment; areas most concerned are:

Energy saving measures
Water saving measures
Green purchasing
Waste minimization practices

Hospitality management associations are paying increased attention to providing the industry with best practice examples and guidelines. An example is the International Tourism Partnership which has produced a set of sustainable hotel sitting, design and construction principles. Another example for the restaurant industry is the American National Restaurant Association which has established a set of guidelines that move the restaurant industry toward more environmentally sound practices and sustainable initiatives. The International Hotel & Restaurant Association (IH&RA) recently realized the need for more sustainable practices and has developed a set of ecological, business smart solutions. Practices they promote include energy, water and other natural resource conservation, increasing recycling and encouraging the use of sustainable materials and alternative energy sources. Founded in 1919, the IH&RA is the leading business association for the restaurant industry. It comprises 945,000 restaurants and food outlets employing 13.1 million people in the United States.

The Green Restaurant Association, a US non-profit, consultative and educational organization with the mission 'to create an ecologically sustainable restaurant industry', also conducts research in various environmental areas. They established several environmental guidelines for restaurants and promote examples of best practice in order to facilitate achieving environmental sustainability. An example is their 'Guide of Endorsed Products', a compendium of environmentally responsible products for the restaurant industry in which they provide information about organically certified, recycled, chlorine free and other environmentally preferable product choices. These examples show that within the hospitality industry, sustainable awareness is growing but is still in its very early stages.

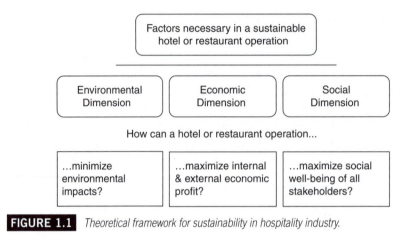

FIGURE 1.1 *Theoretical framework for sustainability in hospitality industry.*

Figure 1.1 provides a pictorial display and a holistic perspective of the theoretical framework for sustainability. Taking the definition of a sustainable hospitality operation, the whole value chain and life cycle of an operation has to be taken into consideration when identifying critical aspects that impact on sustainability. Everything from construction to furnishing, from food and beverage sourcing to production and waste management, to all the various day-to-day operations have to be in harmony with the environment, society as well as operational profitability.

Environmental dimension

The environmental dimension focuses on an organization's impact on flora and fauna that make up the ecosystems in addition to the air we breathe, the water we drink and the land we enjoy. It involves looking at a company's environmental footprint in regard to all its operations, facilities and finished products. Thus, all waste and emission elimination must be examined in detail. Productivity maximization and efficiency of all assets and resources must be strived for. The overall objective is to minimize all practices that might adversely affect the enjoyment of the planet's resources by present and future generations. Avoiding short- and long-term environmental damage and maintaining and promoting natural diversity are the main objectives of this dimension.

Hospitality operations can impact on the environment during building construction, manufacture and use of fixtures and fittings, cultivation of food, as well as when using energy and water or producing waste. This examination of environmental impacts before and during hospitality operations is known as an environmental life cycle analysis.

Economic dimension

All private sector organizations have the main aim of making a profit. They have other aims as well, but if their main aim is not fulfilled, they will sooner or later stop operating. Profit maximization, whether stated as the primary objective or not, is essential for all commercial organizations; without profit they simply go out of business. In recent years, it has become obvious that some practices that contribute to environmental sustainability can also provide significant short- and long-term business benefits. Saving costs through installing energy and water efficient technologies, using energy efficient equipment and ensuring efficient and fair staff practices can increase internal profitability. Additional business benefits of improved relationship with stakeholders, improved staff morale and motivation, enhanced public reputation, increased market share can result from sustainable management systems.

A hospitality company committed to a sustainable business policy supports and participates in the development of the local economy and will aim to generate economic benefits for local people through increased local employment opportunities, business linkages and other income generating opportunities.

Social dimension

The social dimension deals with the impact an organization has on the society within which it operates. The main consideration of the social dimension is how the hospitality operation can positively contribute to the lives of local people in the present and in the future. A company committed to sustainability, therefore, has to deal with issues such as public health, social justice, human rights, labor rights, community issues, equal opportunities, skills and education, workplace safety and working conditions. It must also maintain and promote social and cultural diversity, involving communities, consult stakeholders and the public as well as train staff in regard to sustainable practices.

A hospitality operation needs to be able to assess the social impact of its activities in order to enhance the well-being of individuals and communities. Issues such as fair trade and fair prices in regard to sourcing products and food items require consideration. Local food and beverage sourcing should be considered. Careful attention must be given to food safety issues and human health considerations in regard to the food and beverages offered.

Sustainable competitive advantage in the hospitality industry

A strong motivation for hospitality companies embarking on sustainable business initiatives is the competitive advantage that can be achieved. Although competitive advantages are seen to be necessary, it must be stated that in fast changing macro-economic environment conditions, competitive advantages do not last very long. Furthermore, gaining sustainable competitive advantage within the hospitality industry can be difficult due to the hypercompetition that exists. As in all hypercompetitive industries, rivalry is abnormally high and competition is fierce. In this situation, companies observe very closely the moves of competitors and industry leaders, and immediately copy their successful strategies as they are introduced.

Competitive advantage cannot be gained by only one single improvement; it requires a company to constantly question its strategic position. Thus, competitive advantage through sustainability can only be achieved by constant screening of competitors and constant innovation. It must be emphasized that in this respect technology plays a vital role in increasing competitiveness for a hotel company.

Competitive advantage and technology

Over the last decades, the number of technological patents has vastly increased and technology has become a dynamic energizer of many businesses. Better technology often leads to greater efficiency and shorter product life cycles. Businesses are forced to carefully assess which technologies to put into practice. In addition, new technologies usually require large capital investment and commit companies to using the new technology for long periods. In this process, hotel customers have become more educated regarding technology and their needs have changed accordingly. Hotel guests request the same standard of technology in their hotel room as they have at home.

Technological innovation is one of the most powerful sources of competitive advantage; and applying superior technology has helped many firms to achieve a better competitive position within the hospitality industry.

CASE STUDY 1.1: Eco-Advantage

Eco-advantage

The fundamental idea behind eco-advantage is that the pursuit of sustainable management systems offers opportunities to gain competitive advantages. Hospitality owners and managers are beginning to understand that companies have to stop considering environmental issues as threats and have to realize that sustainable strategies bear huge business opportunities. In the past, companies have been accused of believing there was a fixed trade-off between the economy and the environment. Industry analysts claim that this assumption has resulted in a stalemate. To resolve this stagnation, companies should rather focus on the enormous opportunities that environmentally sustainable business approaches have to offer. These opportunities are to be found in decreased inputs due to a reduction in the use of raw material, higher operating efficiency, increased revenue and an improved company image.

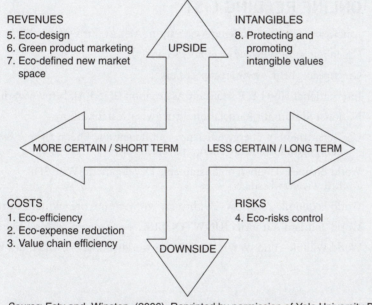

REVENUES
5. Eco-design
6. Green product marketing
7. Eco-defined new market space

UPSIDE

INTANGIBLES
8. Protecting and promoting intangible values

MORE CERTAIN / SHORT TERM   LESS CERTAIN / LONG TERM

COSTS
1. Eco-efficiency
2. Eco-expense reduction
3. Value chain efficiency

DOWNSIDE

RISKS
4. Eco-risks control

Source: Esty and Winston, (2006). Reprinted by permission of Yale University Press. From "Green to Gold: How Smart Companies Use Environmental Strategy to Innovate, Create Value, and Build a Competitive Advantage." by Esty, D.C. and Winston, A.S., 2006. Copyright © 2006 by the Yale University Press; all rights reserved.

Eco-advantage – a strategic approach

This concept builds upon four key pillars: costs, risks, revenues and intangibles. Furthermore, the model distinguishes a downside and an upside. The intention of this model is to decrease the downside (costs and risks) while simultaneously increasing the upside (revenues and intangibles). Hotels that have an environmental program in place can gain advantage over competitors by reducing costs and risks. On the other side are revenues and intangibles. When hotels have implemented sound environmental programs, they have the possibility to market such initiatives to their customers. The marketing of environmentally sustainable products and services is called 'green' marketing. It bears the potential to attract more customers and therefore create additional revenue. Some hotels have made considerable increases in their customer base through green marketing. Having a 'green' brand can be a powerful source for competitive advantage.

CHAPTER QUESTIONS

1. What are the major environmental issues facing humankind in this century?
2. Describe the three pillars of sustainability.
3. Give your opinion whether or not the hospitality industry should become more sustainable.
4. Describe the concept of eco-advantage. How can a hospitality operation improve revenue figures through sustainability?

ONLINE READING LIST

American Hotel and Lodging Association (AHLA): http://www.ahla.com

Greenhotels: http://www.greenhotels.com

Greenpeace: http://www.greenpeace.org

International Hotel & Restaurant Association (IH&RA): http://www.ih-ra.com

National Restaurant Association: http://www.restaurant.org

US Department of Energy Efficiency and Renewable Energy: http://www1.eere.energy.gov/solar/clean_energy_payback.html

World Business Council on Sustainable Development (WBCSD): http://www.wbcsd.ch

World Economic Forum (WEF): http://www.weforum.org/en/index.htm

World Tourism Authority (UNWTO): http://www.unwto.org/facts/menu.html

World Wildlife Fund (WWF): http://www.worldwildlife.org/who/index.html

CHAPTER 2

Energy Efficiency

Study Objectives

- To describe the issues concerning energy consumption in a hospitality operation and define the term carbon footprint
- To differentiate between renewable and non-renewable energy sources
- To describe solar, wind, geothermal, wave, hydro and biomass energy
- To explain carbon offsetting and carbon neutrality
- To describe the process involved in an energy management program
- To describe examples of energy efficient technology

ENERGY USE IN THE HOSPITALITY INDUSTRY

Hotels are the largest consumers of energy not only in building construction but also as establishments with complex installations, which provide guests with high levels of multi-faceted comfort and exclusive amenities, treatment and facilities. Many of the services provided to hotel guests are highly resource intensive whether it concerns energy, water or raw materials. A significant amount of the energy used is wasted leaving ample room for intelligent measures of energy efficiency and conservation. Since the installation of energy-, water- and raw material-saving techniques in hotels can achieve environmental progress and offer competitive advantages to hotels in outperforming their counterparts, many new energy-saving facilities have been introduced by the hotel sector in the past few years following technological advances.

On a worldwide basis, the energy used in hotels is predominantly fossil fuel based or comes from nuclear reactors. A truly sustainable hotel must not only consider ways to use energy wisely but should also consider the possibilities of enhancing the use of energy from renewable sources. Renewable and non-renewable energy alternatives are typically not compared with each other from the perspective of their entire lifecycle impact and cost. With few exceptions, insufficient or no value is attached to the effects of energy use on the quality of the environment, biodiversity, human health and the overall quality of life, all of which would substantially benefit from the enhanced use of renewable energy resources and energy efficient technology.

The carbon footprint is a measure of the impact the activities of individual or business have on the environment and in particular on climate change. It relates to the amount of greenhouse gases produced in our day-to-day lives through burning fossil fuels for electricity, heating, transportation and so on. The carbon footprint is a calculation of all the greenhouse gases we individually produce and is measured in tons or kilograms of carbon dioxide equivalent. In some cases it can be reduced or neutralized by a variety of measures. The first being to reduce dependence on non-renewable energy sources in favor of renewable energy alternatives.

RENEWABLE ENERGY USAGE

There are only two types of energy: renewable which is unlimited and non-renewable which as we all have heard will eventually run out. Worldwide energy consumption for the period from 1995 through 2005 witnessed an average annual growth of 2.4%. The world energy production grew from 34.5 trillion kWh in 1995 to 43.6 trillion kWh in 2005. Oil and oil derivates remained the most important energy sources in 2005 accounting for 36.8% in the total amount of the primary energy sources, although this represents a somewhat lower amount than in 1995 (39.0%). During the same period renewable energy sources in the form of geothermal, solar and wind energies, as well as biomass grew to 370 billion kWh in 2005 but only representing 0.93% in the total world energy production. In 1995, it accounted for 0.6%. (International Energy Agency, 2005)

Renewable energy includes wood or other biomass, wind energy, solar energy, fusion and hydropower. Non-renewable energy includes fossil fuels, coal, geothermal energy and nuclear fission.

Solar power

Passive solar design takes best advantage of natural sunlight and airflow. Buildings with a passive architectural design take into account the daily cycle of the sun shape, the need for artificial light. Cooling and heating can be reduced considerably while creating a comfortable indoor atmosphere. Designing buildings to maximize the use of natural lighting can reduce energy consumption by 40–60% compared to conventional buildings. Traditional day lighting techniques include roof light wells, tall windows and courtyards. Modern alternatives include light monitors, light reflectors or optical fibers used to transport light.

Active solar energy produces limited quantities of electricity or heats water pipes for guest hot water and other applications. Solar energy is not constant, however. In winter, overcast skies, shortened days and long nights restrict the use of solar energy.

Solar water heating is a sustainable source for hot water supply. Usually the collector panels are installed on the roof in order to optimize exposure to sunlight.

Photovoltaic solar panels are the third way to use the energy from the sun. These panels contain solar cells that convert daylight into electricity and can be placed on roofs or can be integrated into the side of the building as sunscreens that can reduce the need for air-conditioning. The electricity produced can either be used directly in the building or in many cases sold to the local utilities company.

Wind power

Wind turbines capture the kinetic energy stored in the wind and convert it into electricity. Wind farms are constructed normally where wind funnels through mountains or hills. Wind power is completely environmentally safe; however, it can be intermittent. Significant power generation requires a good deal of windmills in one farm, thus affecting scenery.

Hydropower and wave power

Hydropower is electrical energy that is generated by using the flow of water through a turbine with a generator, usually derived from rivers or man-made installations. An option for a restaurant operating in a mountain region, where a river or stream provides a continuous source of flowing water, could be a small hydropower system. For hotel properties located on a coastline, wave power may be a future source of energy.

Geothermal power

Geothermal power is energy that is gained by heat stored beneath the surface of the earth. Pumps bringing heat from beneath our feet can be used to directly heat hotels and other buildings or used as a source of power that drives steam turbines to produce electricity. In some places this heat source is close to the surface and can provide a cheap and efficient source of energy. However, in most surface areas bore holes would have to be made to uneconomical depths to bring up the energy.

Biomass

Biomass fuels are produced by converting plants or other biological material into electricity. Biogas is one of the many forms of bioenergy derived from biomass. Biogas is a mixture of methane and carbon dioxide produced by bacterial degradation of organic matter in anaerobic conditions which can be used as a fuel for production of electricity and heat. Organic matter that can serve as a digestate usually comes from some other activity such as agriculture, urban waste, food processing industry, restaurants or any other activity that generates biodegradable organic matter. In Europe, biomass energy production has become one of the standard technologies in the treatment of organic waste, where countries like Germany, Denmark and Austria are leading the way.

While biomass holds promise for hotels to be able to buy electricity created from it, it is very doubtful that stand alone applications of this technology will one day be available. For hotels with a large number of vehicles, the biofuel ethanol can be a viable alternative to petrol.

Main sources of biofuels are energy crops such as maize, rapeseed, crop residues such as rice husks or some kinds of biological waste. It can be used as a solid fuel or be converted into liquid or gaseous forms. Brazil had declared energy independence by producing large quantities of ethanol from sugar cane. An unpleasant side effect of the production is the price of maize which has risen significantly. Since it is the main feed used in beef production and for milking cows, using ethanol to power vehicles might push up the price of beef and milk. Another source of biomass is wood; a hotel might consider installing a convenient wood pellet burning–heating system instead of using oil or gas. Even with so many promising alternative renewable energy sources, hoteliers should not forget that conservation is the key to efficient energy use, no matter what the source of the energy may be.

BUYING GREEN ELECTRICITY

As already explained in previous sections, green energy means energy that has been produced in a more sustainable way. Public utility companies are in some cases beginning to use renewable technologies, such as wind, biomass, geothermal, hydro or solar for electricity generation. This energy is then sold to private users or businesses. A hospitality operation purchasing green energy should refer to labels such as the European Green Electricity Network (EUGENE) label, to ensure that the purchased energy really is green. This independent European Ecolabel guarantees that the electricity comes from sustainable energy sources.

CARBON OFFSETTING

Reducing carbon footprints by purchasing 'carbon offsets' is becoming a popular idea throughout the economy and increasingly in the tourism industry. However, the system of carbon offsetting is controversial, while some feel it is a great solution, others believe that carbon offsets lull people into a false sense of well-being about their ecological impact on the earth. Carbon offset programs essentially allow companies or individuals to 'make up' for the carbon dioxide created by their actions – from creating products or services, driving a car, to the energy needed to sustain a hotel room. Many carbon emissions for the hospitality industry simply cannot be avoided. Guests must fly, drive or take the train to the hotel. The hotel creates carbon emissions, although sometimes small, at all stages of the guest stay including the room where he or she sleeps, the meals eaten, the facilities used and the preparation necessary for the entertainment enjoyed. Even the best consumption reduction programs cannot completely eliminate carbon emissions. To make up for these emissions, hospitality executives and guests can participate in carbon offsetting programs to 'buy' their way out. Carbon offsetting organizations make an estimation of the carbon dioxide created during the hospitality guest stay and attach a price to it. This can be on a departmental basis or an average guest stay basis, a degree of guess work is inevitable in this process since tools that make a precise assessment of carbon emissions are still in development. The funds collected from the carbon offset customers are directed to programs that generate clean energy such as solar arrays and wind farms, which can, in turn, be used to power hospitality operations.

Carbon offset programs are now numerous and they have different methodologies for measuring and verifying carbon emissions; how much should be charged, or even how many kilograms should constitute a legitimate offset. Some projects donate a larger percentage of revenues to actual offsetting projects, while others keep more for their business overheads.

Hospitality executives and guests interested in these programs need to:

- Understand how the program chosen calculates carbon emissions and how they calculate the offsets.

■ Consider the certification for the offsetting program. No universal standards for certifying carbon calculators or carbon offsetting programs exist but the non-profit making organization Clean Air/Cool Planet has produced an annual consumers' guide.

Source: http://www.cleanair-coolplanet.org/ConsumersGuidetoCarbon Offsets.pdf

Steps to achieving carbon neutrality

Step 1: Assess carbon footprint
Step 2: Deduct emissions free electricity purchases
Step 3: Implement emissions reduction measures
Step 4: Compute remaining carbon emissions
Step 5: Purchase offsets
Step 6: Communicate carbon neutrality
Source: Clean Air/Cool Planet

The first of the six steps toward achieving carbon neutrality is to measure the carbon footprint of the hospitality operation, without this data it is impossible to start offsetting or reducing. Step two is to ensure the request for proposal contains a green element. For example, if the property is purchasing electricity from a wind farm that is already carbon neutral, this is deducted from the carbon footprint assessment of the property. Step three establishes the total carbon footprint and in step four negotiations and contracts are made with the carbon offsetting organization. Step six consists of measuring the effectiveness of the carbon offsetting policy and communicating the results to all stakeholders.

Carbon dioxide by the numbers

One ton of carbon dioxide is emitted when you:

■ Travel 2,000 miles on a plane
■ Drive 1,350 miles in a large sport utility vehicle
■ Drive 1,900 miles in a mid-size car
■ Drive 6,000 miles in a hybrid gasoline-electric car
■ Run the average American household for 60 days
■ Graze one dairy cow for eight months

To offset 1,000 tons of carbon dioxide you could:

■ Move 145 drivers from large SUVs to hybrid cars for one year
■ Run one 600 kW wind turbine for an average year
■ Replace 500 lightbulbs of 100-watt with 18-watt compact fluorescent lights

- Replace 2,000 refrigerators with the highest-efficiency model
- Install 125 home solar panels
- Plant an acre of Douglass fir trees

Source: Clean Air/Cool Planet

From the Hospitality business perspective participating in carbon off-setting schemes makes sense because a growing number of consumers are impressed by companies that demonstrate environmental stewardship. This form of eco-advantage is not negligible in a rapidly changing economy. Since many carbon offsetting projects are located in developing countries, this action raises the ethical profile of the hospitality company. Lastly, no one yet has all the solutions to solving all the issues of environmental degradation. Although carbon offsetting may not be the perfect solution it does allow individuals and companies to be at the cutting edge of experimental and innovative approaches to solving these issues.

CASE STUDY 2.1: Carbon Neutral Hotel

Rufflets Country House Hotel, St. Andrews, Scotland
Working with The Carbon Neutral Company, the hotel under-took a full audit of its energy usage, not simply in terms of electricity and gas, but also the additional consumption, including business mileage (by car, train or airplane) and also fuels used in the upkeep of the grounds and gardens. The result of this audit was that the business was generating 273 tonnes of carbon emissions annually (based on figures from January 2006 to January 2007), and the offset cost, amounting to over £3,000 was invested in 3 projects, linked with Scotland and tourism. Rufflets officially announced carbon neutral status in June 2007, becoming one of the first carbon neutral hotels in the UK and the first in Scotland to do so.

The three investment projects were as follows:

Reforestation: South West Scotland – 20% of the offset was invested in the re-forestation project currently under way in Dumfries. However, it is recognised that the full impact of this will not materialize for a few decades.

Energy Efficiency: Jamaica – a country that does not have its own natural resources, and imports vast quantities of diesel fuel to run generators producing electricity for its main income stream – tourism. 40% of the investment will be used to help a fund that will increase the number of energy efficient programmes in the country, such as low-energy lightbulbs.

Renewable Energy: New Zealand – a wind farm project, certified as being Gold Standard, on the North Island, it is the first in the country to use the new megawatt-class machine!

Basically, this means that each turbine can produce enough electricity to power 900 homes, giving greater diversity in generation, reducing greenhouse gases and other harmful emissions.

The owning partners of Rufflets have committed to continue to audit the emissions annually, with the main emphasis on reducing the current levels, but also to offset the amount of CO_2 produced into new projects each year.

Carbon Neutral Objective: It is accepted that the business will always use gas and electricity, and therefore produce CO_2 emissions, but the initial aim is to reduce the overall usage, and the cost of the offset. As the offset cost decreases year-on-year, the owners will use the monetary difference saved to re-invest into eco-business programmes, with the long-term view to be recognised as showing 'best practice' within the industry.

Source: http://www.rufflets.co.uk/rufflets_hotel/carbon_neutral_hotel .html

THE USE OF ENERGY IN HOTELS

There are substantial differences in energy use between different types of hotels depending on hotel size, class/category, number of rooms, customer profile (business/vacation), location (rural/urban), climate zone in addition to the types of services/activities and amenities offered to guests.

A hotel can be seen as the architectural combination of three distinct zones, all serving distinctly different purposes:

- The guest room area (bedrooms, bathrooms/showers, toilets) individual spaces , often with extensive glazing, asynchronous utilization and varying energy loads

- The public area (reception hall, lobby, bars, restaurants, meeting rooms, swimming pool, gym, sauna etc.) spaces with a high rate of heat exchange with the outdoor environment (thermal losses) and high internal loads (occupants, appliances, equipment, lighting)

- The service area (kitchens, offices, store rooms, laundry, staff facilities, machine rooms and other technical areas) – energy intensive requiring advanced air handling (ventilation, cooling, heating).

Typically, about half the electrical energy is used for space conditioning purposes. According to the US Environmental Protection Agency, there are 47,000 hotels that spend $2,196 per available room each year on energy which represents about 6% of all operating costs.

Depending on the category of the hotel, lighting may account for up to 20% or even more. The demand for domestic hot water varies appreciably with hotel category ranging from 90 to 150l or sometimes more. Supplying domestic hot water accounts to up to 15% of the total energy demand. For a medium category hotel with an average annual occupancy of 70% this is the equivalent to 1,500 to 2,300 kWh per room. Catering and other facilities also account for an important share of overall energy use. By comparison, operating elevators, pumps and other auxiliary equipment account for only a small percentage of total energy expenditure. Through a carefully managed strategic energy management approach to energy efficiency, a 10% reduction in energy consumption would have the same financial effect as increasing the average daily room rate (ADR) by $0.62 in limited-service hotels and by $1.35 in full-service hotels (Energy Star, 2009).

There is a widespread misconception in the hospitality industry that substantial reductions in energy used can only be achieved by installing advanced, high-maintenance and prohibitively expensive technologies. While this may be true in some contexts, in the majority of cases major energy savings can be achieved by adopting a common sense approach, requiring neither advanced expertise nor excessive investments. When first embarking on an energy management program, the first step is to establish exactly how much energy is being used and in which way. This is achieved through an energy audit.

ENERGY AUDITING

An energy audit is the systematic review of each fuel, and energy consuming system in the establishment. It commences with the collection, and analysis of all information that may affect energy consumption and inspects the condition and performance of existing systems, installations, existing management techniques and utility bills. The findings are then compared to the energy performance published standards (benchmarks) in other similar establishments and proposals are made. An energy audit is not an excuse for cutting energy consumption, rather managing the usage to maintain and or improve hotel guest and worker comfort. An annual energy audit is much like an annual accountants review, stating the past and current energy balance.

ENERGY CONSUMPTION GOAL SETTING

Once a clear picture of energy consumption is created, goals for improvement can be made. Measurability is an important key to the success of an energy management program and helps the establishment to identify progress and setbacks at operational level. A clear energy program that embodies attainable goals demonstrates commitment to reducing environmental impacts and has a motivational effect on staff and guests.

The energy management team should create departmental targets and establish a tracking system to monitor progress. This system should also embrace time lines for actions including regular meetings with personnel to discuss completion dates, milestones and expected outcomes.

DEFINING AND IMPLEMENTING AN ACTION PLAN

Determine which members of staff should be involved and what their responsibilities will be. For an energy management program to succeed, the support of all personnel is required with leadership coming from the top. Specifically, some departments will have certain responsibilities; finance – capital investment and budget planning; human resources – training and performance standards; supply management – procurement procedures, energy, equipment and material purchasing. For each part of the action plan, estimate the cost for each item in terms of both human resources and capital/expense outlay. Develop the business case for justifying and gaining funding approval for action plan projects and resources needed.

Staff warrants recognition when results are reached and accomplishments should be highlighted. Tracking sheets, scorecards, bonuses and prizes can be motivational. Good communication stimulates interest amongst stakeholders and commitment amongst staff. All information on energy use, environmental impacts and energy-saving options should be published for the general audience of the establishment's web site and in the local news media.

CASE STUDY 2.2: Hotels Making a Difference

After receiving the Energy Star Partner of the Year Award in 2005 and 2006, Marriott International's company-wide continuous improvement in energy management helped the organization win the prestigious Energy Star Sustained Excellence designation in 2007. In 2006 alone, Marriott was able to save almost $6 million and reduce its greenhouse gas emissions by 70,000 tons. The program included the installation of 450,000 compact fluorescent light bulbs (CFLs), conversion of all outdoor signage to LED and fiber optic lighting, and implementation of energy- and water-efficient laundry systems. Through its reduction in energy consumption, Marriott's efforts represent a 2 percent greenhouse gas reduction per room – well on the way to the corporate goal of 6 percent savings per available room by 2010.

Source: Energy Star: http://www.energystar.gov/ia/business/challenge/learn_more/hotel.pdf

ENERGY EFFICIENCY TECHNOLOGY

Heating, ventilation and air conditioning (HVAC)

Depending on the hotels' geographic location, HVAC can account for up to 50% of a hotel's total utility costs: electricity, water, gas and fuels. The latest generation of air conditioners consumes up to 30% less energy than those manufactured 20 years ago. Modern chiller units not only save energy but are even able to recover the heat they produce during operation. The heat, which is normally expelled to the atmosphere can now be used to pre-heat water for laundry or swimming pools, thus, creating savings.

Not only has air-conditioning technology been improving over the past decades, but also heating systems have become more efficient, requiring less maintenance. Air conditioning units, called heat pumps, can now supply hotels with hot air as well as cold air. Geothermal heat pumps are similar to ordinary heat pumps, but use the ground instead of outside air to provide heating, air conditioning and, in most cases, hot water. Because they use the earth's natural heat, they are amongst the most efficient and comfortable heating and cooling technologies currently available.

Probably the most efficient system of heating is gas fired condensation boilers. They are capable of converting 88% of the fuel used into heat, whereas older models only achieve 80%. Those recent boilers contain a second heat exchanger using the heat that would usually escape through the chimney. Hotels seeking a very effective and comprehensive energy solution might choose to invest in the new combined heat and power systems which work like mini power stations converting gas into electricity, heat and hot water. These systems are advantageous because their combustion efficiency is only about 10–20% less efficient than fuel burning public power stations and they also produce less carbon dioxide and sulfur because they run on gas.

Intelligent room functions

Thanks to the application of new technologies which enable rational use of energy, hospitality companies can reduce power consumption per night. Using so-called intelligent hotel-room systems, electricity can be saved by adjusting air conditioning, heating and lighting systems according to the guest's presence in a room. Some hotels have sought benefits in this area by interconnecting the hotel's energy management system with its property management system to ensure consumption reduction when a room is unoccupied. The linking of energy use and room occupancy presents a natural synergy for conservation. At the time of checkout, all non-critical equipment in a guest room can be automatically controlled or turned off. Items such as alarm clocks and refrigerators are not affected, while thermostatic controls, television sets, select room lighting and related components might well be subject to a power-down condition.

Additional energy-saving initiatives for HVAC:

- Limit thermostat control in guest rooms and public areas
- Use outdoor air for cooling where possible
- Ensure heating and cooling cannot be provided simultaneously
- Regular maintenance to optimize efficiency

- Install curtains to control solar heat gain
- Sun shade oriented windows with awnings
- Insulate hot/chilled water tanks, pipes and air ducts
- Insulate the entire building correctly
- Zone guest occupancy and turn off heating/cooling on unoccupied floors

Source: http://www.energystar.gov

Day light and electric light

One way to greatly enhance the thermal performance of windows is to install Low-E glass. i.e. glass that is manufactured with a microscopically thin and transparent layer of metal or metal oxide that reflects infrared 'heat' energy back into the building.

Electric lighting is another element of the hotel guest experience that is affected in many different ways. However, with lighting costs accounting for an estimated 20% or more of total energy usage, energy-efficient lighting can help reduce energy consumption costs. Energy efficient lighting has sometimes been characterized by low-quality lighting, with poor color rendition. Recent lighting technology is radically changing all this. Compact fluorescent lights (CFLs) use about 75% less energy than standard incandescent bulbs and last up to 10 times longer. CFLs provide the greatest savings in fixtures that are on for a substantial amount of time each day. For this reason, they are typically used in guest rooms and corridors as well as back of the house. Due to major improvements over the last few years in their color rendering abilities, CFLs are now a viable alternative to incandescent lamps.

Where color options or different effects are desired, LED lighting is now a good choice. Light-emitting diode (LED) bulbs can provide bright lighting as well as increasingly better color rendition with less energy use. Typical uses include cove lighting in corridors, display lighting and increasingly different alternatives as the technology continues to expand rapidly. LEDs last from 100,000 hours to 1,000,000 hours compared to a 30,000 maximum life span of fluorescent bulbs, plus they do not contain the harmful mercury found in fluorescent bulbs.

Additional energy-saving initiatives for lighting:

- Adjust lighting levels to demand and types of fixtures
- Use time and motion sensors for turning off lights where appropriate
- Use dimmer controls in dining and public areas
- Clean bulbs and reflecting surfaces regularly for maximum efficiency

CASE STUDY 2.3: Hotel Operation Energy Practices

The Rezidor Hotel Group

Operating hotels involves the use of raw material, energy and water, and results in waste generation. Rezidor's main environmental impacts are a result of energy use and the consequent contribution to climate change, in addition to consumption of materials.

In 2008, the Rezidor Hotel Group committed to tripling the number of hotels with third-party environmental certifications to ensure hotels are doing their utmost to reduce these impacts. The focus of these certifications is on concrete savings, better indoor environment, waste management, energy efficiency, environmental training of employees and informing guests about the Responsible Business programme.

The Rezidor Hotel Group energy consumption consists of electricity, district heating and cooling, heating oil, natural gas, and LPG gas. Energy costs as a share of Rezidor's total costs is 4.2 % (4.6), and during 2008 the Hotel Group spent TEUR 23,771 (23,304) on energy related costs for leased hotels. Rezidor is committed to contributing to mitigating climate change by continuously improving the energy-efficiency of the operations and by increasing the share of carbon-neutral energy sources. Over 49% (50) of hotels responded that they undertook some kind of environmental investment during 2008. The vast majority of these investments are related to energy saving measures. These measures include the installing of sensors and motion detectors as well as low energy demand equipment, upgrade of heating and ventilation systems, and performance of energy audits. The majority of hotels also reported immediate savings or cost avoidance achieved due to these investments.

Energy Efficiency in Practice

Challenge: The Radisson SAS Hotel, Leeds, has five levels of guest bedrooms and each corridor has approximately one hundred compact fluorescent lights.

The result is a very bright environment and high energy consumption.

Response: In 2008 the hotel changed one corridor to LED light fittings and the effect has transformed this level dramatically – giving a new modern look to the hotel corridor while maintaining an adequate amount of light for the guest's comfort. The engineering team managed to retain and reuse the original compact fluorescent fittings by inserting a standard GU10 fitting inside the original. This has reduced the cost of the project so that the project was fully completed by the end of the year on budget and moreover with no additional cost, as the LED lights are priced almost the same as compact fluorescents. The hotel estimates that just one refitted corridor will result in a saving of 18,000 kWh on consumption. In addition the hotel will save on the monthly purchasing of compact fluorescent lights and on man hours required for the hotel engineer to do daily light replacement rounds, as LED have a life span of 50.000 hours – far greater than that of compact fluorescents. This results in a total calculated saving of at least 5,000 per year and the hotel has already begun to expand this project throughout the hotel in areas such as guest restrooms to further reduce consumption.

Source: Sustainability Report of The Rezidor Hotel Group (2008)

CHAPTER QUESTIONS

1. What is the difference between 'carbon footprint' and 'carbon offsetting'?
2. Describe what is meant by solar power, wind power and biomass energy.
3. How can carbon neutrality be achieved?
4. How much carbon dioxide would you be responsible for emitting if you drove your mid-size car from Los Angeles to New York and then flew to London?
5. Describe the steps in an energy management program.
6. What are intelligent room functions?

ONLINE READING LIST

Clean Air Cool Planet: http://www.cleanair-coolplanet.org/

Energy Star: http://www.energystar.gov/

European Green Electricity Network: http://www.naturemade.ch

Green Energy Standard EUGENE: http://www.eugenestandard.org/

International Energy Agency: http://www.iea.org/

US Environmental Protection Agency: http://www.epa.gov

CHAPTER 3

Waste Management

Study Objectives

- To explain the impacts of waste on the environment
- To describe the various forms of waste
- To explain how waste can be reduced
- To explain how product design can reduce waste
- To explain a strategic approach to reusing waste
- To give examples of ways to recycle waste

WASTE AND THE ENVIRONMENT

The hospitality industry can become an important actor in the minimization of waste that is currently hauled off and disposed of at landfill sites. The industry can be active in the creation of recycling centers and programs, using environmentally friendly cleaning supplies and techniques and sourcing locally produced goods and services that reduce transportation expenses. As in other businesses, the top priority in the hotel industry is maintaining high guest satisfaction. Thus, there is great concern that any environmental improvements or conservation methods implemented will not negatively affect customer comfort and satisfaction. Most people are familiar with the traditional definition of waste management, which basically concentrates on the removal of rubbish from a private dwelling or business premises. In the hospitality industry, the scope of this definition continues to evolve as operators begin to embrace the three 'R' 's of reuse, recycling and reduce. Probably the newest component in this equation concentrates on the latter, reducing the amount of waste operations produce in the first place.

The European Union produces 1.3 billion tons of waste each year. In other words, 3.5 tons of refuse and liquid or solid waste per European citizen, nearly a third of this food waste for which the food service industry has a responsibility. Another 40–45 million tons of this huge mountain of waste is classed as hazardous, or particularly dangerous. Among other things it can be:

- *Persistent* or non-biodegradable which remains dangerous for a long time e.g. plastic bottles and tin cans.

- *Bio-accumulative*, which accumulates as it makes its way up the food chain e.g. some chemical pesticides and herbicides.

- *Ecotoxic*, which causes damage to the environment e.g. improperly treated used engine oil.

- *Carcinogenic*, which causes cancer e.g. asbestos.

Every kilo of waste equates to inefficiently used resources, in addition, the disposal of waste has to be paid for usually directly by the hospitality operation in the form of a tipping fee. In some cases, the establishment has to pay a haulage fee to have the waste transferred to a municipal landfill site, a transfer station or a recycling center.

Although there are costs involved in recycling processes, every cardboard box or plastic bottle recycled saves the amount of energy that would have otherwise been used to make it from virgin material. Waste disposal is not an efficient or clean business. Even though standards are improving, waste management facilities are still significant polluters. Aside from the problem of illegal dumping, badly managed landfill sites are a source of pollution; non-biodegradable rubbish for future generations; releases the greenhouse gas methane into our atmosphere and damage the landscape. Incinerated rubbish can contribute to air pollution if incorrectly handled, likewise recycling and composting vegetable material can also pollute if badly run.

Within the hospitality industry, food and beverage operations account for a substantial amount of waste. This waste can be defined as:

- Pre- and post-consumer food waste, packaging and operating supplies. Pre-consumer waste is defined as being all the trimmings, spoiled food and other products from kitchens that end up in the garbage before the finished menu item makes it to the consumer.

■ Post-consumer waste, naturally, is any rubbish left once the customer has consumed the meal.

■ Packaging waste, especially in the form of plastic that cannot biodegrade naturally, as anything used to hold food coming into the kitchen and going out. Operating supplies encompass every other piece of material used that becomes wasted in a foodservice operation, such as cooking oil and light bulbs.

Waste is classified as biodegradable (vegetal and animal matter) and non-biodegradable (inorganic matter: plastics, glass, metal). In addition, hotels produce so called biological wastes (human sewage) and ashes if an incinerator is used in the establishment. Hazardous wastes that are normally associated with heavy industry and also with manufacturing industries are also present in hotels and restaurants. They include the solvents used in paint and floor finishes, the chemicals used in some cleaning products and batteries that contain heavy metals such as mercury. Every effort must be made to either avoid using such products or, if they are indispensable, they should be dispose of correctly.

Another, new and worrying waste is the category known as E-waste (electronic waste) coming from computers, mobile phones, fax machines, copiers, etc. Although fairly harmless while in use, these devices contain an assortment of heavy metals such as lead, mercury and arsenic that are difficult to separate. Since recycling is difficult and expensive in terms of time, this waste is often sorted by people in developing countries working in unsafe conditions who sacrifice their health to do it. The remainder ends up in municipal landfill and accounts for an estimated 40% of heavy metals found in municipal landfill sites.

Manufacturers are coming under mounting pressure from legislators and consumers alike to minimize their impact on the environment, leading to the design for the environment concept. This embodies all manner of issues, such as reduced energy usage, transportation, packaging, recycling and waste reduction and disposal. Emerging from the design for the environment concept manufacturers are now trying to embody the principles of design for disassembly (DFD).

The aims of DFD are to design a product that can be readily dismantled at the end of its life and thus optimize the reuse, remanufacturing or recycling of materials, components and sub-assemblies.

CASE STUDY 3.1: Talking Rubbish

Hilton Hotels, meanwhile, is focusing on another method: rubbish recycling. It is following in the footsteps of the Hilton Glasgow, which slashed hotel waste to 49 tonnes between November and January. The bins were 24 tons lighter than the same period the previous year, after the hotel installed colour coded recycling bins for paper, glass, oil and food. The group plans to do the same for its other 72 properties in the UK and Ireland. According to Matt Todd, project manager at the Centre for Environmental Studies at Oxford Brookes University, the 'tide has turned' in the last year for green issues in the hospitality industry.

'Many of the things hotels do you won't notice, like closing windows, turning the heating down a degree and switching off lights. These cost and energy saving measures are happening across the industry,' he said.

Source: Travel Trades Gazette, (March 2007), www.ttglive.com

ECO-PROCUREMENT MINIMIZING WASTE

Eco-procurement or eco-purchasing considers not only the traditional specifications of quality, price, delivery, availability, convenience, etc. but also considers the disposal of the item and its packaging after use. Eco-procurement works with the principles of DFD. Alternatives to disposable plastic cutlery and plastic plates are carefully considered, most ecologists would argue that plastic has no part to play in food service. As a midway between plastic utensils and Styrofoam take-away containers a new generation of compostable packaging is entering the market place. World centric products made from 'agrifibers' (such as sugarcane pulp) and 'bioplastics' (made from various plant starches) are being used in place of the usual paper and Styrofoam packaging. Some of these products can be used in the dishwasher and are microwave safe, all are biodegradable.

WASTE REDUCTION TACTICS

Management should work with suppliers to procure products that promote waste prevention. Some suppliers may be able to change products and packaging to reduce the waste the hotel manages. For example, ask food service vendors if they can deliver items in reusable shipping containers. Consider buying or leasing used or remanufactured furniture, fixtures and equipment. Typical remanufacturing operations performed by suppliers are replacement of worn parts, refinishing of metal or wooden surfaces, repairing of scratches, dents and holes, and reupholstering of cushions. Extending the life of furniture, fixtures and equipment through remanufacturing reduces the rate at which they are discarded. Purchasing in bulk, using recycled products and buying from suppliers that have a proper environmental policy in place, are all measures that help to reduce the amount of waste generated. Moreover, buying products with a longer lifetime will also lead to decreased waste.

Creating less waste or eliminating waste before it is created means creating less pollution and saving natural resources. This can be done by working together with suppliers and encouraging them to reduce their packaging, reuse packaging or change to reusable packaging where possible. Purchasing some items in bulk may be another option for reduction, cleaning materials, for example, can be purchased in concentrated form and mixed in the hotel. Many hotels now supply guests with liquid soaps and shampoos in refillable ceramic containers in the bathrooms. Outsourcing can sometimes help hotels to reduce waste and cut costs. Services such as dry cleaning that require an important capital expenditure and that if badly managed produce hazardous waste should be considered carefully. Alternatives, such as using a local company could be more cost effective and result in less pollution.

Reduce: a strategic approach

We have all been in hotels where we are asked whether we would like to have our towels and sheets replaced daily, or whether we wish to 'help the environment' by reusing them. In many ways this typifies the early approach to hotels wishing to green their credentials. Although many other ways have now been developed to 'help the environment', reducing laundry is still a worthy gesture. Besides saving water and energy, reduced laundering will also cut down on the use of detergent and bleach. According to the US National Association of Institutional Linen Management, hotel laundry costs range from $3 to $4 per day per room. It is estimated that hotels can save up to $1.50 per day per room by reminding guests they have the option of choosing not to get freshly laundered sheets and towels each day of their stay.

Many foodservice managers are horrified at the amount of food left on plates. American and European cities have wrestled with excess food waste for more than a decade but in Hong Kong where shrinking landfill space is a growing concern, the city elders are pushing the inhabitants to adopt a new consumption ethic. In the past five years, the amount of food wasted by Hong Kong's restaurants, hotels and food manufacturers has more than doubled, according to the Environmental Protection Department (EPD). In an attempt to change wasteful dining habits one of Hong Kong's 'hot pot' restaurants that offer 'all you can eat' for a fixed price are charging HK$5

(US64 cents) per ounce for leftovers. In another sushi restaurant, the owner charges HK$10 (US$1.28) per leftover sushi. Restaurateurs are often loathe to reduce portion size in the fear of losing customers, however, by offering 'come back for seconds' options some restaurants are managing to reduce the overall amount of food waste.

Cooking to order, rather than bulk food cooking can also reduce waste even though labor costs may increase. Often in canteens food that is cooked in bulk and held for a period of time, such as soups, hot entrées, pastas and other foods are thrown away if not consumed. Tracking food waste can work as a useful deterrent. When culinary staff are trained to weigh food trimmings and other pre-consumer waste at the different food preparation stations in the kitchen using special scales as part of a waste management system, the foodservice manager is able to pinpoint where most of the food waste is coming from. This attention to detail makes the staff more mindful of their cuts during food preparation and reduces excess trimmings going into the dustbin. Management can also introduce incentives for those staff members who produce the least waste.

Reuse: a strategic approach

Another strategy is to reuse as much as possible of the waste generated. This means finding ways to use the waste from one process as the raw material for another one. Reusing material is a better choice than recycling, incineration or landfill. Reusing differs from recycling in that recycling breaks down an item into its basic parts and makes a new product out of it, but reusing an item keeps the material in its original form and uses the item over and over again for the same or different purposes. There are many examples of reuse in the hospitality industry; here are just a few that are applicable to both restaurants and hotels regardless of their type and size:

1. *Reusing textiles* – convert damaged textiles, such as uniforms and linens, into useful items. For example, torn bed sheets, towels and banquet linens into reusable guest-room laundry bags, baby bibs, crib bumper pads, aprons, cleaning rags and bar covers either by the establishment itself or by a charity organization. Another possibility: repair torn bed linen and reuse it on smaller cots or cribs. Replace single-use items with reusable items such as napkins, tablecloths and hand towels. When they are worn, turn them into cleaning rags. Dye-stained towels a darker color for reuse at the pool or beach, or as cleaning cloths. Extend the useful life of curtains by rotating them to expose different portions to sunlight.

2. *Reusing containers* – means that less material is needed to manufacture containers, and there will be less material requiring recycling and disposal. Reuse of packaging can also save money for companies that either ship or receive products by reducing the cost of packaging, disposal and product damage due to shipping and handling. In addition, companies report that they have generated additional long-term cost savings by implementing reusable container systems, including reduced freight, labor, and handling and storage costs.

3. *Reuse bottles and glasses* – hotel and restaurant operators can choose from a wide variety of options when they purchase and dispense beverages. For example, beer can be packaged in kegs, cans or bottles. Bottles are either intended to be reusable or to be used just once, after which they are disposed of or recycled. In some countries like Germany, using reusable bottles is a way of life in other countries throwaway plastic bottles and glasses are the norm. A bottle that is filled 20 times eliminates the need for making 19 more bottles, avoiding not only the need to dispose of those 19 containers but avoiding also the environmental effects of material extraction, processing, manufacturing, distribution and recycling.

4. *Reusable food* – donate edible, unused food to local charities. Many hundreds of programs throughout the European Union and the US accept food-packaged, fresh, frozen or baked – that restaurants and hotels can no longer use. Donor programs deliver food to soup kitchens, homeless shelters, senior citizens' programs, day-care centers and food pantries. If possible, collect unusable food scraps and arrange to have them picked up by local pig farmers for use as animal feed. First, check with the local health department or cooperative extension office, as some countries and municipalities do not allow the feeding of food scraps to animals. Used deep fryer oil is now used successfully by motorists who have modified their car engines to run on this cheap fuel.

Recycle: a strategic approach

A recycled product describes a product that is made entirely or partly from secondary material recovered from consumer waste. Some products are reduced to their raw state and remanufactured into something resembling their original state. In the case of recycled paper, the newspapers gathered from guest bedrooms and the used notepaper coming from the hotel copy shop are reduced back to their raw state of paper pulp which is then used to produce more paper. Unfortunately, many products recycled in this manner come back as lesser quality products. Paper comes back as packaging material or paper towels. This process is known as downcycling, plastic is another such product. When the used plastic is melted down it looses strength because its long polymer chains of molecules are sheared. This recycled plastic can be made into building bricks or blocks, commonly used successfully in developing countries but if made into plastic bags the result is more flimsy than the original product. For some products, downcycling is not a problem such as metals and food waste. Aluminum can be used over and over again without any loss of its original qualities. As in the case of all metals, there is a considerable cost saving from recycling aluminum and no additional damage.

Recycling is becoming big business as the volume of waste increases. According to European Union statistics, the amount of municipal waste produced in western Europe increased by 23% between 1995 and 2003, to reach 577 kg per person. In Europe, some countries, such as Austria and the Netherlands, now recycle 60% or more of their municipal waste. The recycling rate in Britain stands at 27% and in the United States 32%. Both countries have seen a considerable growth in the last few years.

According to the Stern Review, commissioned by the UK government in 2006 which assessed the economic challenges of climate change, the idea of recycling remains a noble one, and it makes eco sense; recycling plastic saves 2 tons of CO_2 in comparison to incineration and recycling paper economizes 1,400 kg of CO_2 per ton. Even exporting recycled material provides around five times the savings in carbon emissions compared to sending it to waste for energy treatment facilities (WRAP, 2008).

Sending the European consumers' rubbish to China in container ships has made headline news in recent years and promoted a knee jerk reaction of condemnation from ecologists. Research has shown that sending plastic bottles and paper for recycling in China actually saves carbon emissions. Shipping these materials more than 10,000 miles produces less CO_2 than sending them to landfill in Europe and using brand new materials. According to the UK government funded association WRAP, Waste & Resources Action Programme in 83% of circumstances recycling paper, card, glass, plastics and metals is preferable to any other option for dealing with them. Recycling these items is estimated to save more than 18 million tons of greenhouse gas emissions per year in the United Kingdom alone.

Recycling has other advantages. It conserves natural resources, saves energy and reduces greenhouse gases and pollution that result when scrap materials are substituted for primary raw materials. If recycled materials can be used, ore does not have to be mined, trees cut and oil does not have to be drilled as much. Extracting metals from ore, in particular, is extremely energy-intensive especially aluminum extraction. Using recycled aluminum can reduce energy consumption by as much as 95%. Savings for other materials are lower but still substantial: about 70% for plastics, 60% for steel, 40% for paper and 30% for glass. Recycling also reduces emissions of pollutants that can cause smog, acid rain and the contamination of waterways.

Unfortunately, there is a threat to recycling in the form of declining commodity prices and in our market economy the two are undeniably linked. It seems unfair that environmental protection is linked to market prices. However, in 2009 prices have begun to stabilize, even though, in the present economic climate markets are still fragile. Some recyclables – such as glass – have hardly been touched by the price reductions and the demand for glass remains strong. Using recycled glass saves 25% of the energy that would have been used to make a product from new materials. Very few people now disagree with the idea of recycling and are happy to participate in these programs. Most people accept that we live in a world of finite resources and that communities across the planet need to work hard not to exhaust the resources that society has yet to plunder.

PLAN TO REDUCE WASTE

The departmental organization of hospitality operations is challenging when establishing a recycling program. The company must provide organizational resources, the most important being enthusiasm. Giving the responsibility of leading the program to the right person or people is the main key to success. The following guidelines will help any hospitality company that has decided to put into place a recycling program:

- *Decide on leadership*, who will be the Recycling Program Manager, who will be in his or her team. This person might already have a position in managing operations; essentially the person must be an organizer and an enthusiastic communicator who can win support throughout the business.

- *Analyze waste streams*, do a waste audit. The act of counting and measuring, although tedious, focuses attention. Many hospitality professionals have stories of checking waste bins and pulling out perfectly useable utensils and crockery that have been dropped in by mistake. Decide how waste is to be separated and set up disposal systems with local municipalities or recycling companies. Not only for raw materials like paper, glass, aluminum, etc. but also for fixtures and fittings. Charity organizations are only too happy to take household items.

- *Establish an accounting system* that reflects monthly waste management costs. A monthly report is needed for tracking waste disposal and recycling information. Create recycling goals for departments and waste material reduction. Organize projects and activities that involve the personnel and that incidentally bring positive publicity to the establishment.

- *Build ownership* by involving employees at all stages of the program. Post the goals on bulletin boards so all employees are informed.

- *Close the loop*, that is to say, buy recycled products. Recycling programs need evaluation periodically and refinement if goals are not being reached. Most recycling programs need stimulation from caring members of staff.

Composting

Pioneering initiatives can help the environment and result in positive publicity for the business. There are examples of restaurants that transform kitchen and garden waste into useful compost. Compostable items i.e. food that cannot be donated, come in many forms, non-fatty waste including spoiled fruit and vegetables, stale bakery items, kitchen preparation trimmings and leftover plate scrapings. Compost bins are used for the process and the active partner in the enterprise is *Eisenia foetida* or the red wriggler worm which is smaller than worms normally found in the garden and will work 24 hours per day 7 days a week to transform kitchen waste into rich black loam (humus). An added advantage of composting is that unlike rubbish dumps where organic matter produces the greenhouse gas methane, using worms for composting prevents this by turning waste into stabilized organic matter.

CASE STUDY 3.2: Vermiculture to Reduce Hotel Waste

The Mount Nelson Hotel is a luxury hotel in Cape Town. The hotel is an urban sanctuary, situated within a sprawling lush garden estate in the heart of the city's vibrant cultural centre and close to the waterfront and beaches.

The Mount Nelson Hotel recognises the pivotal role such an operation plays in a community. Therefore the hotel is dedicated to working towards the conservation of South Africa's natural resources and in educating the staff to make a difference in the lives of others. The Mount Nelson Hotel has many onsite eco-initiatives including the establishment of an on-site 'worm farm' (or vermiculture centre) to process leftover food and other organic matter into compost, which is used to fertilise the hotel's gardens.

Vermicompost is the heterogenous mixture of decomposing vegetable or food waste. Vermicompost can be mixed directly into the soil as fertilizer. The benefits of Vermiculture are multifaceted:

Soil: Vermicompost enriches the soil with micro-organisms

Plant growth: It improves root growth and structure

Economic: It reduces waste flow to landfills. It also requires a low capital investment and uses relatively simple technologies.

Environmental: It recycles waste onsite.

Source: http://www.mountnelson.co.za/web/ocap/in_house_conservation.jsp

CHAPTER QUESTIONS

1. What are the different types of waste?

2. Why is waste a problem for the environment?

3. Discuss the concept of design for disassembly.

4. What is eco-procurement and what can be done to reduce waste?

5. Discuss ways of reusing items that would normally be considered as waste in a hotel.

6. Discuss ways to recycle waste.

7. Do you think composting is a possible alternative for disposing of vegetable waste in a restaurant?

ONLINE READING LIST

Environment Green: http://www.environment-green.com

Hong Kong Environmental Protection Department: http://www.epd.gov.hk/epd/eindex.html

How to compost: http://www.howtocompost.org

Association for Linen Management: http://www.almnet.org/

Stern Review: http://www.sternreview.org.uk

US National Association of Institutional Linen Management: http://www.osha.gov/dcsp/alliances/nailm/nailm

Waste & Resources Action Programme (WRAP): http://www.wrap.org.uk/downloads/LCA_of_Management_Options_for_Mixed_Waste_Plastics.54c64a6f.5497.pdf

Water Conservation

Study Objectives

- To explain the issues of water conservation
- To describe the need to consider water availability in the hospitality development process
- To explain water conservation techniques in hotels
- To describe some examples of modern water saving technology
- To give examples of pioneering ways to cut down on water use
- To explain the use of 'green' detergents

WATER CONSERVATION: PROBLEM DEFINITION

Much is said about the need for the global community to reduce its carbon footprint but humankind needs to address another ecological imbalance, its 'water footprint'. A third of the world's population must contend with severe water shortage and many western countries are struggling against depleting aquifers and increasing water needs for which modern lifestyles are partly to blame. It is not only the increasing world population that is increasing demand but also our cravings for garden pools, consumer products and a richer diet of more meat, fish and milk.

According to the US Environmental Protection Agency it takes 39,090 gallons of water to manufacture the average new car and its tyres and nearly 4l of water to process a hamburger. As countries like China and India move away from agrarian economies where meat eating was exceptional rather than the norm, great strain is put on diminishing water resources. The water required for a meat-eating diet is twice as much as is needed for a 2,000-liter-a-day vegetarian diet. Even more pressure is being put on dwindling water supplies where new crops are developed in the name of environmental preservation to produce biofuels. Although, in global terms, water is a precious and diminishing commodity, many users see little incentive to conserve it because its price is negligible even though it is in constant escalation. Global warming is predicted to put further pressure on water resources with serious consequences for countries lying in the temperate latitudes.

The hospitality industry and tourism in general present a number of challenges for the management of water supplies. The most popular tourist destinations are located in regions with warmer climates and low rainfall, especially during the peak tourist season. Mediterranean climates are the most badly affected in this respect. Moreover, such countries often have a natural predisposition for drought. The annual influx of tourists increases the demand for water well beyond the normal requirements of residents and the possibilities of local water sources. On a per capita basis, hotel guests and tourist activities demand more water than local residents.

In tourist destinations and regions, there is often a geographical dimension to water supply. Hotels and tourist facilities are normally concentrated in coastal areas away from the main sources of surface water that are often in more remote upland locations. Thus, water supply and demand are usually mismatched seasonally and often dislocated geographically from one another. In the Mediterranean basin, overexploitation of local surface water sources and aquifers, to meet these demands is lowering groundwater tables. Saline intrusion i.e. seawater contamination can result in coastal areas where water tables fall below sea level. This leads to the destruction of fauna and flora habitats, resulting in a less attractive ecology for visiting tourists and the local population. Hence, water is essential to the sustainable development of tourism and the hospitality industry.

Creative solutions to solving water shortages in tourist areas have been to ship water in from far away and to produce drinking water from seawater i.e. desalination. Many Mediterranean islands have to be supplied from the mainland due to water scarcity. Water tankers supply many of the Greek islands on a daily basis and at one time the Spanish island of Majorca was supplied by water coming from the Ebro Valley in Catalonia, in north-eastern Spain. The scheme was abandoned after a few years due partly to the expense but also because of opposition from the population in north-eastern

Spain. The local population in Ebro Basin protested at the extraction of 'their' water supplies and environmental problems caused to the wetlands of the Ebro delta.

Compared to freshwater from rivers and groundwater, desalination requires large amounts of energy, usually in the form of fossil fuels, as well as specialized expensive infrastructure. In Dubai, as in other Middle Eastern countries, desalination is used to provide most of the regions' needs in water. In fact, the rapid development of the United Arab Emirates has been made possible due to the desalination plants powered by cheap fossil fuel. During the process large quantities of brine are produced that are normally pumped back in the sea. Critics point out the high costs of desalination technologies in terms of the energy required and the marine pollution when the brine is pumped back into the oceans at high temperatures.

WATER CONSERVATION IN HOTELS

Water conservation is perhaps not the first issue that crosses a hospitality manager's mind when making out the management agenda. Issues such as revenue management, marketing and personnel are prioritized. However, from the perspective of the guest, the use of water is an integral part of his or her experience. Water restrictions would result in unhappy guest stays and so maintaining adequate water comfort must be central to all water management strategies. Purchasing water and the disposal of dirty water are becoming increasingly expensive activities. Issues of water scarcity push up prices, and as profit margins in the hospitality industry are relatively small, the astute manager's attention is becoming focused on this subject.

Any water use reduction program must have the full support of the staff. Some hotels have estimated that only a small percentage of water consumed is actually by the guest, the remainder is used by the chambermaids during cleaning. Water is a crucial resource for the hospitality industry as it is a limited resource and is needed for a number of activities as depicted in Figure 4.1.

As with energy, the approach toward decreasing water consumption is to regularly train staff on how they can contribute with simple measures toward decreased water consumption. In contrast, Webster (2000) warns that water policies should not have a negative effect on a hotel's hygiene and cleanliness.

The attention of all staff needs to be focused on water consumption, repairing small leaks that produce immediate gains, hundreds of litres of

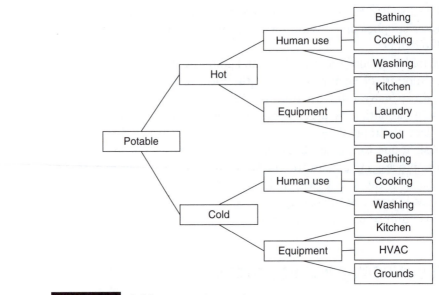

FIGURE 4.1 *Building water systems and uses.*

water can be lost each week in a toilet cistern that is not functioning properly. While more than half of water consumption in hotels takes place in guest-rooms (guest showers, sinks and toilets), kitchen operations, laundry and public areas represent the remainder of total water consumption. In addition to staff awareness and correct training, water metering on each floor gives employees a clear indication of how much is being used. It allows the hotel to set up clear benchmarking systems.

Water conservation in hospitality operations is achieved as in the management of waste; reduce, reuse and recycle. All water management systems should not affect guest satisfaction.

WATER USE REDUCTION IN HOSPITALITY OPERATIONS

The first step in water management is an efficiently designed and maintained plumbing system. A gravity fed cold- and hot-water system delivering low-pressure water uses less water than a mains pressure hot-water system. Reducing the water pressure from 100 to 50 pounds per square inch (psi) can reduce water use by approximately one third. Such a system might be practicable in lodges and guest houses situated in rural areas but in large hotels guests are used to high-pressure showers.

Sinks and showers

Conventional twist taps use around 4l per hand wash; water-efficient fixtures can reduce this to 2l or less. Flow-controllers or low-flow fixtures can be installed in plumbing where water pressure is less important as in food preparation areas and public toilets. This technology can also be used in showerheads and for baths if the management wishes. Further reductions can be achieved by implementing tap aerators. These spray devices create fine water jets that incorporate air and reduce water flow to 5l per minute. Showers in public areas like spas and pools should be equipped with push buttons that limit the water flow to a certain duration. A novel way of encouraging guests to stay in the shower for less time is to place an egg timer in the shower with signage inviting guests to monitor their time spent. The latest generation of sink taps are equipped with infrared sensors that automatically turn off when a person walks away or when the allotted quantity per wash has been delivered. Again, this system is fine for public areas but can be inconvenient in guest rooms where a hand has to be waved in front of the light to keep it flowing.

Toilets and urinals

Another, water intense facility within hotel bedrooms are toilets and urinals. Conventional flush toilets are responsible for up to 40% of domestic water use. Putting a displacement device or a tank restrictor in the cistern will reduce the cistern capacity but a more efficient solution is to fit a low-flush toilet that uses less than 4l of water per flush, cutting water use in half. There are many different models including: dual flush toilets, with a lower flush option for fluids and a standard flush level for solids; gravity toilets, that depend on gravity alone; and pressure assisted toilets that combine gravity with compressed air.

Eco-tip: Dry composting toilets

Dry composting toilets and urinals are the most water-efficient toilets on the market, using no water at all. They use biological processes to deal with the disposal and processing of human excrement into organic compost material. Waste is transported to a composting chamber below the toilet by gravity; vacuum-flush systems can flush horizontally or upward. There are also commercial systems that use a small amount of water 'micro-flush', usually about 0.5l per use. All work on the same principle: waste material in the toilet is composted in a separate chamber with no interruption of the process, no unpleasant smell and minimal exposure to unprocessed material. Compost-toilet systems are beginning to compete with and replace conventional toilets in public facilities. One example is in the University of British Columbia, Canada, in the C.K. Choi Building which contains 5 compost chambers with 12 toilets for 300 full-time employees. Additionally, they produce nutrient-rich compost for use in the establishment's garden.

Modern water flush urinals are equipped with passive infrared sensors that ensure an economical amount of water is used to flush the urinal after each use. Even better are urinals that do not need to be flushed at all, they are coated with nano-particles creating a hygienic film. A cartridge placed at the bottom of the urinal acts as a funnel directing flow through the liquid sealant, preventing any odors from escaping. This cartridge collects sediment and allows the remaining waste to pass freely down the drain.

CASE STUDY 4.1: The THC Rotorua Hotel in New Zealand

In many water assessments, urinals and automatic flushing toilets are found to consume a great deal of water. The THC Rotorua Hotel in New Zealand had urinals that flushed automatically every nine minutes. Each flush used 10 liters of water. This added up to 66 liters per hour, or 1,580 liters per day, regardless of whether the urinals had been used or not. The total consumption for three urinals was 4,740 daily. The hotel then installed detectors that sense when the urinals are being used and allow flushing to occur at a specified time after use. This programme reduced water consumption in the three urinals from 66 liters per hour to 40 liters during the day and to 20 liters in the evening. In addition to installing the urinal sensors, the hotel installed low-flow showerheads at a cost of $3,060. The annual cost savings for the water conservation came to $5,244, with a payback of only seven months.

Source: Auckland Regional Council available at http://www.arc.govt.nz/environment/managing-pollution-and-waste/waste-and-recycling/environmental-accommodation-providers-of-auckland-eapa/water-conservation.cfm#THC

Laundry

Hotels that operate on premises laundries have several options to reduce water consumption. The first is to use front loading machines that consume less water and less detergent than top loading models. Front loaders also have improved spinning performance and extract more water, thus, reducing drying times. A further way to reduce laundry is guest participation in towel and linen programs where guests have the option to use the same sheets and towels for more than one day. Most guests appreciate these initiatives although in five-star luxury hotels some managers report guest resistance and are reluctant to apply reuse programs.

Swimming pools and spas

Warmer water evaporates more quickly than cooler water, keeping the pool cooler will slow evaporation. However, this measure could seriously affect guest comfort and satisfaction and should be instituted with care. Pool covers will also reduce evaporation and have the added advantage of reducing heat loss in cooler climates.

Eco-tip: Natural swimming pools

Natural swimming pools work on the same principles as ponds and lakes to produce clear and clean water. Natural swimming pools are purposely built to use nature's purifying properties of plants and micro-organisms to produce perfectly healthy swimming water. The basic difference between a natural pool and a conventional swimming pool is the latter uses chemicals such as chlorine to kill bacteria. Plants and natural organisms are used in natural swimming pools to completely eliminate impurities and bacteria and the need for chemicals and constant cleaning. Natural swimming pools have the added advantage of being a water feature in the grounds of the hotel.

Gardens and water features

Water conservation is important in good garden maintenance. In an attempt to create a prestigious and luxuriant landscape around the property some owners unfortunately use plant varieties that require constant artificial watering. The first rule must be to plant indigenous plant species where possible that are best adapted to the local climate and soil conditions. Such varieties will also save on fertilizers and pesticides. Grass is an example that in many areas requires much attention and is highly water and fertilizer intensive. Many properties over water simply because employees do not understand what the plants require. Watering should also take place either early in the morning or late in the day to reduce the possibility of evaporation in hot weather. Properties investing in fountains and water features should turn off appliances at night and consider the use of graywater.

Eco-tip: Wastewater recycling

Graywater and blackwater are the two kinds of wastewater produced in all buildings and hospitality operations. Graywater comes from baths, sinks, showers and kitchens and can be recycled and reused for watering the garden or flushing toilets. Blackwater comes from toilets, and contains harmful pathogens. It must be properly treated before being discharged into the environment. Reusing graywater for flushing toilets can save up to 50% of domestic water use, but requires some form of treatment such as filtering and disinfectant to remove bacteria and other biological material. If used directly for watering the garden, graywater can be left untreated, but only biodegradable non-toxic household cleaning and toiletry products should be used in the water system. Great care must be taken if using water coming from restaurant kitchens as fats and other additives might be present resulting in the need for a more sophisticated treatment. Both blackwater and graywater can be effectively recycled on-site using constructed wetlands or reed bed systems.

Eco-tip: Rainwater collection systems

Rainwater can be collected from roofs, from driveways and other paved areas, and then after being filtered it can be channeled into a cistern or rainwater tank for storage. This water is then used in the garden, or for toilet flushing. Collected rainwater can be used in evaporative cooling equipment for air-conditioning (likewise seawater) or for fire protection systems. Installing point of use water heaters ensures that cold water is not wasted while waiting for hot water to come through the taps. Well-lagged and properly positioned pipes will also help keep water hot. Along with plumbing design, water conservation is achieved through the specification and installation of water-efficient appliances and fittings.

CASE STUDY 4.2: Greener Cleaners

Operators explore how eco-friendly cleaning products benefit not only the greater good, but also the immediate kitchen environment.

Generally speaking, a cleaning product is green if it biodegrades and doesn't contain petroleum-based chemicals and harsh synthetic compounds. As a result, green cleaners have fewer toxic chemicals and tend to be more pH neutral, attracting the attention of operators from independents such as The Kitchen to chains, including 20-unit, New York City-based Le Pain Quotidien.

Still, changing products and practices takes a step-by-step approach. Le Pain Quotidien found that purchasing biodegradable containers for takeout and implementing water-efficient spray valves was easier than changing to all-green cleaning products. There are challenges for operators looking to bring in green products. Jim Solomon, chef-owner of The Fireplace Restaurant in Brookline, Mass., has been more than satisfied with an all-purpose, biodynamic natural cleaner he recently began using. But he admits that many green products aren't as restaurant friendly as they could be. 'The quality has risen; the price has come down quite a bit. And now it's an implementation issue,' he says. In addition, 'you've brought an extra vendor into the mix'.

Michael Ehlenfeldt, general manager of Stone Hearth Pizza's locations in Belmont and Sudbury, Mass., recently switched to an unscented, biodegradable hand soap and hopes to find a green degreaser. In the meantime, he monitors the quantity of chemical cleaners his staff uses and challenges reps to find greener products, hoping that as the chain grows, his buying power will ease the process. Hugo Matheson, chef and co-owner of The Kitchen in Boulder, Colo is more than familiar with the difficulties of finding the right product. 'Cleaning is one of the hardest things to deal with in a restaurant,' he says. His bottom line shoulders

CASE STUDY 4.2: (Continued)

some of the challenge. Last year he paid $50 for a gallon of hand-washing soap designed for home use. He's remedying the situation by working with his soap provider to develop a natural, unscented hand soap he can purchase more economically. 'We continually have dialogues with suppliers and slowly it changes,' Matheson says. As evidenced with hand soap, there are simple ways to start using greener products. Matheson suggests that smaller restaurants start with hand soap and floor cleaner. 'Go to a hardware store and pick up the largest container of eco-friendly floor cleaner and try it,' he suggests. Ehlenfeldt has another simple approach. He dilutes vinegar with water in a spray bottle and uses it for light cleaning. 'It costs about a buck a gallon,' he says.

Source: Kate Leahy, Restaurants & Institutions, 2/1/2007: http://www.rimag.com/article/CA6521398.html

CHAPTER QUESTIONS

1. What are the issues surrounding water availability in tourism and hospitality developments?
2. What are the environmental problems caused to communities and tourist developments when water becomes scarce?
3. Describe the process of desalination.
4. Describe how hospitality managers can reduce water consumption with the use of technology.

READING LIST

Energy Saving Trust: http://energysavingtrust.org.uk

Green Hotels: Opportunities and Resources for Success: http://www.zerowaste.org/publications/GREEN_HO.PDF

International Tourism Partnership: http://www.tourismpartnership.org/

Saving Water: http://savingwater.org/business_hotels.htm

US Environmental Protection Agency: http://www.epa.gov/

Webster, K., 2000. Environmental Management in the Hospitality Industry. Cassell, New York.

CHAPTER 5

Eco-Design in Hospitality Architecture

Study Objectives

- To explain the impacts buildings and hotels have on the environment
- To describe the waste created and the resources used in the construction of a hospitality operation
- To describe principles of sustainable architectural design
- To explain the priorities of sustainable design
- To explain the theory of embodied energy
- To describe sustainable certification and rating systems for buildings

CONTENTS

The hospitality industry constitutes one of the most energy and resource intensive branches of the tourist industry. Energy efficiency in facilities designed for hospitality is frequently low and the resulting environmental impacts typically greater than those caused by other types of buildings of a similar size. The negative effects on the environment during the construction phase are caused by the excessive consumption of non-renewable resources e.g. water, electricity and fuel, as well as by emissions into the air, groundwater and soil.

Many hospitality travelers demand more from hospitality facilities. They expect a high level of comfort and service in accommodation and food and beverage operations, they also desire experiences that cater to their needs and wants. In addition, the modern guest wishes to feel that his or her actions are environmentally responsible, they wish for an earth-consciousness experience that will ensure their hospitality stay caters both to them and the world in which they live. The concepts of service and ecology once appeared to be polar opposites in the hospitality industry. The traditional idea shared by both the consumer and the property was that, in introducing more sustainable and environmentally friendly alternatives, the property would sacrifice ambience, comfort and the guest's enjoyable experience. Thanks to technological advancements and greater environmental knowledge, this is no longer so. In the majority of cases, major energy saving can be achieved by adopting a common sense approach requiring neither advanced expertise nor excessive investments. This is particularly true when the concepts of energy efficiency and resource conservation are accounted for already when planning and designing a hotel facility. In recent years, this process has become known as eco-design, green design or sustainable design.

IMPACTS OF BUILDINGS ON THE ENVIRONMENT

The construction industry is one of the most conspicuous forms of economic activity. During a building's existence, it affects the local and global environments via a series of interconnected human activities and natural processes. At the early stage, site development and construction influence the local ecology and landscape. The procurement and manufacturing of building materials impact the global environment. Once built the building inflicts a long-lasting impact on the environment. For instance, the energy and water used by its inhabitants produce toxic gases and sewage; the process of extracting, refining and transporting all the resources used in the building operation and maintenance also have numerous effects on the environment.

As a society's economic status improves, its demand for architectural resources – land, buildings or building products, energy and other resources – will increase. This in turn increases the combined impact of architecture on the global ecosystem, which is made up of inorganic elements, living organisms and humans.

CONSTRUCTION WASTE

The construction industry is one of the most highly energy intensive of all industries. It creates large amounts of CO_2 emissions, pollution and waste and uses most non-energy related resources. The UK Association for Environment Conscious Building (AECB, 2009) estimate that building use in the United Kingdom contributes about 50% of the CO_2 emissions and the construction industry contributes about another 7%. The AECB have shown that the Government figures on energy performance of houses grossly underestimate the CO_2 gains that could be made by building energy efficient buildings. According to the UK Department for Environment, Food and Rural Affairs (DEFRA, 2009), the waste going to landfill from the construction industry in 2004 was about 100 million tons or more than three times the amount of domestic waste collection (28 million tons). In many situations this is equivalent to one house being buried in the ground for every three built.

The construction industry is the major consumer of resources of all industries in the United Kingdom. It accounts for 90% of all non-fuel mineral use, and a large proportion of timber use. Many of the materials used in the United Kingdom now come from abroad, sometimes from countries with less environmental control or labor justice. As the World Wide Fund for Nature have shown in their One Planet Living material, if everyone in the world consumed resources at the same rate as we do in the United Kingdom it would take the equivalent of three planets now to sustain this consumption (WWF, 2009).

Resource use in construction

In all western nations, the construction industry is the main consumer of non-renewable resources, as well as a huge consumer of renewable resources that means that it must take responsibility and become more sustainable. Another issue with the construction industry is habitat destruction which can have an immediate and disastrous effect on certain localized areas and species. Sometimes the impact can be global, for example, the impact of the destruction of tropical rain forests to satisfy the demand for construction timber.

The number of species made extinct increases every year as well as the further erosion of biodiversity and rare habitats that happens. Many essential materials are now in short supply. These include materials such as copper, where whole landscapes have been destroyed in South America in the search for rare resources. In Madagascar, the same situation occurs in the quest for titanium, an ingredient of paint. It is therefore imperative that demand on such materials is radically reduced, this entails using less of these materials by building more simply, with more local and plentiful (i.e. sustainable and renewable) materials and with less waste.

Pollution from the construction industry

Finally, the environmental impact of construction is also felt in terms of pollution. This is not in the extraction but in the processing of materials for construction. And again, not surprisingly, the construction industry has the biggest effect of all sectors because of the quantity of materials used in construction. In the past, there was a simple general equation between the amount of pollution and the amount of energy in a process. On the whole the more energy required, and the more processes, the more waste and the more pollution was generated.

Although the processing of many products like plastics, the manufacture of titanium dioxide, the galvanizing of metals are all potentially very polluting, much of this is now controlled by legislation in western nations. Most basic materials and components are now often processed elsewhere. The loss of control of manufacturing processes therefore has a considerable environmental impact. As with habitat destruction, it is difficult to track or control it. Until there is a clear global legislation or certification, the construction industry needs to stick with what is inherently non-polluting.

SUSTAINABLE ARCHITECTURAL DESIGN

The goal of sustainable architectural design is to find architectural solutions that guarantee the well-being and coexistence of society, the environment and profitability. Not only does sustainable architectural design attempt to reduce negative effects on humans and on the environment but it also attempts to create greater resource efficiency than found in conventionally constructed buildings. Efficiency means that these buildings save costs in terms of energy, and water, while providing at least the same ambient quality. Sustainable architecture can be divided into three main parts. The first being sustainable planning. This means that before construction the planners and architects must consider all environmental and social impacts. Social impacts can be health, safety, comfort, productivity or quality of life. To assess these impacts the so called Social Impacts Assessment (SIA) has been developed. In order to assess the environmental impacts an Environmental Impact Assessment (EIA) is made. Conducting an EIA includes identifying direct and indirect impacts, assessing the significance of these impacts, identifying measures in order to avoid or reduce them and establishing strategies for monitoring the success of impact avoidance and reduction.

The principles of sustainable architectural design
The effect of the sun
A fundamental principle of solar design is that the warming effects of the sun's rays should be maximized in the winter and minimized in the summer. This can be achieved in three ways: glazing, orientation and thermal mass.

Controlled glazing is the vital component of environmental design. Although glass allows 90% or more of the energy in the sun's rays to pass through it is a very poor insulator. Double glazing is twice as good (or half as bad) because the small air gap between the sheets of glass is a good insulator. Even so, double glazing still only has the insulating power of a single layer of bricks.

Glass has to be used with precaution, having enough glass to benefit from the free heat of the sun and let in plenty of daylight, but not so much that the house overheats during sunny days and freezes at night.

There are two keys to this problem – orientation and thermal mass.

Orientation

Correct orientation of the building is crucial for determining the amount of sun it receives, because the direction and height of the sun in high northern latitudes and low southern latitudes changes dramatically throughout the year.

- Only surfaces facing south receive sun all year round. For this reason, solar panels and windows that will capture solar warming in winter, should face as close to south as possible.

- Surfaces facing north are in the shade all year round. For this reason solar design concentrates insulation and minimizes glazing on this side of a house.

- The winter sun is low, the summer sun is high. Vertical south facing windows work best for maximizing solar heating in the winter as they capture the low winter sun.

- The high summer sun makes it easy to design shading for vertical windows. Only a small overhang is needed to completely shade a vertical south facing windows in summer. This is another strong argument for maximizing south facing glazing.

Thermal mass

The way in which a building can store and regulate internal heat is known as thermal mass. Buildings with a high-thermal mass take a long time to heat up but also take a long time to cool down. As a result they have a very steady internal temperature.

Buildings with a low-thermal mass are very responsive to changes in internal temperature – they heat up very quickly but they also cool down quickly. They are often subject to wide variables in internal temperature.

Brick, concrete and stone have a high-thermal mass capacity and are the main contributors to the thermal mass of a building. Water has a very high-thermal capacity, so it is well suited to central heating systems. Air has a very low-thermal capacity – it warms up fast but cannot stay warm for long. Only when the walls and floors in a building have warmed up will the air stay warm.

Sustainable buildings are designed to have a high-thermal mass for several reasons:

- To hold over daytime solar gain for night time heating.

- To keep houses cool during the day in summer.

- To increase the efficiency of central heating system. A small boiler working at maximum efficiency will slowly and steadily raise the temperature of the building with high-thermal mass then turning itself off for a long period. Buildings with a low-thermal mass tend to have much wider fluctuations in temperature, and the boiler is constantly switching on and off to compensate. The positioning of exterior wall insulation can affect the thermal capacity of a house significantly.

Stack effect

Air expands and rises when it warms in a process called convection. In this way heat moves around rooms and entire buildings. Ventilation with fresh air is vital and convection plays a leading role in natural ventilation. Hot air rises and escapes through small gaps in the building fabric at the top of the house. Escaping warm air draws in new cold air through similar gaps at the bottom of the house, this is called the stack effect, or sometimes the chimney effect because it is the same process that draws smoke up a chimney. Badly controlled, the stack effect can produce unwanted cold drafts. However, when carefully controlled, it can produce a low and effective level of natural ventilation. The stack effect is by far the most effective way of keeping a building ventilated in summer. Over the past 10 years sustainable architecture has paid increasing attention to generating stack effect to create natural ventilation, especially in large buildings like hotels.

Embodied energy

Sustainable design encapsulates the principle of embodied energy or hidden energy i.e. the quantity of energy required to manufacture and supply to the point of use, a product, material or service. In the case of sustainable architecture the extraction, processing, manufacture and transport of the materials needed in the construction of the building need to be examined.

The embodied energy in the structure of a new hotel is considerable, exceeding the total energy required to heat that hotel for the next 20 years. No hotel can claim to be an eco-hotel if it is constructed from materials that had a major environmental impact elsewhere.

The principle of embodied energy divides new eco-buildings into two distinct groups. The first group of eco-buildings, which at present account for those hotels built along the principles of sustainable architecture, aims at low-energy consumption with the most efficient available technology, such as solar water heating panels and photovoltaic panels that produce electricity. Such buildings have a high-embodied energy which they try to justify with large savings in their energy consumption, or even by becoming a producer of surplus energy that they can supply to others. The other group of eco-buildings such as some eco-lodges aims to achieve the lowest possible embodied energy by using salvaged building material or simple local materials (straw bales, compacted earth bricks, wood-fiber boards, sheep wool, wood frames with wattle and daub) (Table 5.1). Such buildings usually have a higher annual energy consumption and are less durable, but often have a lower overall environmental impact over the course of their lifespan.

Embodied energy in existing hotel properties

Renovating an existing building will always use less energy than building a new hotel. Even if a new hotel is extremely energy efficient, it will be many years before it can pay off the energy embodied in its structure. Alternatively, an existing building only has to account for the embodied energy of the materials used for the renovation in its environmental impact analysis. Renovating existing buildings can also positively reinforce conservation and preservation of buildings with cultural or historical value.

Table 5.1	Coefficient of Embodied Energy of Building Materials (Energy Needed to Produce a Given Material)
	Material Coefficient
Wood	1
Brick	2
Cement	3
Glass	4
Fibre glass	7
Steel	8
Plastic	30
Aluminum	80

In comparison to using new buildings, it can sometimes be more challenging to use redesign techniques and technology when renovating. Especially when the building has evolved over time, there are often restrictions due to historic status, making an environmentally friendly approach more complicated to implement. However, 'greening' existing buildings provides a great opportunity to cut down on energy consumption and carbon emissions. There are always some technologies available that can be used to improve the environmental performance of old buildings, such as a more efficient heating, cooling or ventilation systems.

Other ways to reduce the cost of embodied energy in renovations

- *Use local raw building material*; where possible use local raw building material such as local stone or wood from environmentally managed forest.

- *Avoid materials that have the highest embodied energy*; such as laminated beams, chipboard and hardboard that are bonded with formaldehyde especially materials coming from far away that embody transport generated energy costs.

- *Use salvaged materials*. Using salvaged materials obtained locally from demolition sites or salvage yards effectively cutting out embodied energy altogether other than transport.

SUSTAINABLE DESIGN PRIORITIES

Economy of resources

By economizing resources, sustainable architecture reduces the use of non-renewable resources in the construction and operation of buildings. Economizing energy has highest priority in the eco-hotel because the use of non-renewable energy resources has the greatest environmental impact in the average building. So, when there is a limited budget and a conflict of interest, energy conservation should be prioritized. As an added bonus money is saved in the process. The eco-hotel aspires to self-sufficiency and the more it can meet its own needs, the less of a demand it is making on the wider environment. Examples of self-sufficient technologies include: solar space water heating; using waste gray water and rain water; saving and reusing waste heat; electricity generation from windmills and photovoltaic solar panels. A hotel that reduces its consumption is a highly efficient low-cost building. It is when the hotel starts meeting its own needs that it becomes a true eco-hotel.

Life cycle design

Traditionally, building materials were reused in times gone by. When a house came to the end of its natural life the stones, bricks, wood and sometimes fittings were used to make new houses and other useful buildings for humanity. The conventional building life cycle is now a linear process consisting of four major phases: design, construction, operation and maintenance, and demolition. Environmental issues related to the procurement and manufacturing of building materials or waste management are not addressed. A "cradle-to-grave" approach recognizes environmental consequences of the entire life cycle of architectural resources, from procurement to return to nature. Life cycle design is based on the idea of reusing and recycling architectural materials with no end to their potential usefulness.

Design for humanity and the environment

Design for humanity and the environment is concerned with providing harmony for all constituents of the global ecosystem, including humankind, the flora and the fauna. This principle is founded on the humanitarian principle of the respect humankind has for their neighbors but also for the planet. It is deeply rooted in the need to preserve the ecosystems that allow human survival. Building construction must be limited to improving human life within the carrying capacity of resources and ecosystems. Sustainable architecture is about providing built environments in hospitality operations that provide guests with comfort and provide workers with optimal conditions for productivity.

In the context of sustainable development, hospitality ventures must strive to create optimum relationships between people and their environments. Sustainable development should have the absolute minimal impact on the local, regional and global environments.

RATING SYSTEMS FOR SUSTAINABLE BUILDINGS

LEED

The US Green Building Council (USGBC, 2009) created the Leadership in Energy and Environmental Design (LEED) in the late 1990s. The aim of this green building-rating program is to certify and rate buildings on their environmental performance. The LEED system rates the building construction, design, the use of materials and the use and consumption of energy. Of all the sustainability categories under review, energy resources account for the largest block. When a company or organization applies for certification it has to follow a set of guiding principles. Over the years LEED has become one of the most accepted and well-known international green building-rating systems with more than 2,500 rated properties worldwide in more than 30 countries all over the world.

CASE STUDY 5.1: The Right Environment: A Look Inside the Orchard Garden Hotel

Only a handful of newly constructed US hotels have gained LEED certification from the US Green Building Council. On the green front, the hospitality industry has historically lagged behind fastmovers like corporations, schools and universities. But now, more and more hotel owners recognize the financial, environmental and branding benefits of the reliable LEED green rating.

One of the nation's newest LEED-rated hotels is the Orchard Garden Hotel in San Francisco near the Chinatown Gates. The property is the sister hotel of the nearby award-winning Orchard Hotel. The 10-story, 86-room hotel, which opened in November 2006, was constructed to meet green standards with: the selection of recycled products for many interior finishes, the installation of energy-saving lighting and water-conserving plumbing fixtures, enhanced air ventilation, the selection of sustainably grown wood for furniture, and the use of paints, glue, carpets and varnishes that are made of non-toxic materials and have reduced 'off-gasing.' 'The hotel's owner and executive team built San Francisco's first green hotel for several reasons,' says General Manager Stefan Muhle. 'LEED-certified buildings have lower operating costs, higher employee productivity, and happier and healthier occupants. The hotel's owner, too, is passionate about clean green environments.' Constructing a green hotel presented some challenges. 'While offering organic

cotton sheets would have been a nobrainer, finding sturdy enough cotton was nearly impossible,' Muhle continues. 'We also considered sustainably raised bamboo flooring, but it would have worn out too quickly in high-traffic areas.'

The Orchard Garden Hotel's owners recognized that operating a green hotel does not stop with constructing and furnishing the actual building. The hotel has adopted operations policies, technologies, and supplier relationships that achieve green – and bottom-line – benefits. The hotel uses citrusbased cleaning products which are just as effective as chemical-based products, but do not expose staff or guests to harsh chemicals, or dump those chemicals into the sewers. Each guestroom has recycling bins, and the hotel is 100 percent tobacco free. The hotel also has plenty of traditional guestroom amenities including LCD flat panel TV, DVD and CD player with surround sound, and high-speed Internet and Wi-Fi access. The Orchard Garden has also adopted the first keycardactivated lighting, heating and ventilation system in San Francisco. 'That feature cost $30,000 up front,' Muhler notes, 'but it will certainly pay for itself quickly by saving us up to 20 percent in energy bills per year.'

Source: http://www.theorchardgardenhotel.com/images/press/Green-Retrofit-Lodging-Magazine-02-07.pdf

BREEAM

The Building Research Establishment Environmental Assessment Method is a voluntary measurement-rating system for green buildings established in the United Kingdom. Similar in conception to LEED and Green Star in Australia, and HQE in France. Until now, BREEAM has certified more than 100,000 buildings (BREEAM, 2009).

IS HOSPITALITY LUXURY COMPATIBLE WITH THE ENVIRONMENT?

Hospitality luxury and the environment once appeared to be poles apart in the hospitality industry. The traditional idea shared by both the consumer and the property was that environmentally friendliness was synonym to flickering neon lights in the bedroom and vegetarian nut cutlets in the restaurant. Thanks to technological advancements and creative ideas, this is no longer so. An increasing number of major hotel brands have realized and accepted that the changing luxury market demands that their hotels offer both environmental accountability and a true high-class experience. New, specifically branded, environmentally friendly, five-star properties are now opening. Starwood Capital Group's announcement regarding its new '1' Hotel and Residences brand is a notable entry into this eco-luxury category. Eco-luxury starts with sustainable design and architecture. Hospitality architects and designers are now integrating environmental design into their practices. Whether by developing LEED-certified buildings through the USGBC or just carefully inspecting materials and employing a holistic design strategy, the hospitality industry is moving forward.

Sustainable design does not reduce the guest experience, on the contrary, it can be seen to often enhance the ambience and comfort of the property through, for example, natural light and ventilation. Furthermore, many

CASE STUDY 5.2: Luxury Going Green

The Orchid Hotel in Mumbai, India is a luxury five-star hotel with 245 rooms. Since the opening the hotel earned more than 60 national and international awards and has been certified as the world's first Ecotel with the ISO14001 standard.

The hotel's environmental performance started with the building of the hotel. The façade of the hotel was built out of special, natural fiber cement increasing insulation against the heat. A large swimming pool was installed on the roof, which helps to insulate the building very effectively. In addition the atrium was equipped with natural lighting, which saves a huge amount of lighting costs. Additionally, the hotel was constructed so that 72 rooms are constructed to face the atrium. This also allows a reduction of cooling costs, as these rooms are not facing the sun directly.

Throughout the hotel energy and water saving devices have been installed. The walls are made from fertilizer waste and all windows are triple glazed to decrease heating and cooling costs. The hotel employs a water conservation system and has very effective waste management strategies. The list of sustainable featured items such as coat hangers, and bedroom slippers that are 100% ecological and are made out of recycled materials.

This hotel is one of the best examples of an effective application of sustainability in hotels where the quality of the stay is not jeopardized (Orchid Hotels, 2008).

Source: http://www.orchidhotel.com/mumbai_hotels/awards.htm

no sensory impact on the perceived luxury experience. These behind-the-scenes solutions include lower energy use and power consumption, innovative wastewater technologies and natural paints and building materials.

Eco-luxury branding is about the basics: sustainable materials and processes; a conscious knitting together of resources and the empowerment of everyone from employees to local artisans and businesses. In the case of new buildings, greener construction and design practices that range from the carpeting and external ceiling systems to the light bulbs and washing machines can all come to define eco-luxury. Not only is eco-luxury common sense, it is also now a common expectation.

CHAPTER QUESTIONS

1. What are the environmental impacts and especially of hotels on the environment?
2. How can the building construction process be said to be polluting?
3. Describe the principles of sustainable construction.
4. Why are there less environmental impacts during the renovation of a building than in construction?
5. Explain the sustainable design priorities.

ONLINE READING LIST

Association of Environment Conscious Builders (AECB): http://www.aecb.net/index.php

Association pour la Haute Qualité Environnementale (HQE): http://www.assohqe.org/

Building Research Establishment Environmental Assessment Method (BREEAM): http://www.breeam.org

Department for Environment, Food and Rural Affairs (DEFRA): http://www.defra.gov.uk/

Green Building Council of Australia (GBCA): http://www.gbca.org.au/

Leadership in Energy and Environmental Design (LEED): http://www.usgbc.org/DisplayPage.aspx?CategoryID=19

United States Green Building Council (USGBC): http://www.usgbc.org/

World Wildlife Fund (WWF): http://www.panda.org

CHAPTER 6

Sustainable Food and Beverage Management

Study Objectives

- To explain what is sustainable food
- To describe the issues around food security and genetic engineering
- To define the categories of sustainable food
- To explain the issues of nutrition and health
- To explain the challenges of modern food production
- To describe organic food and organic food labeling
- To explain the concept 'food miles'
- To explain how sustainable wine can be sourced

CONCEPT OF SUSTAINABLE FOOD AND BEVERAGE MANAGEMENT

According to the Worldwatch Institute (2009), the major problem in the global food production system is in the unsustainable inputs that are used. As a result, many forms of environmental degradation occur; falling water tables, deterioration of pasture, soil erosion. The western diet, with its high consumption of fish, meat and dairy products is endangering the environment; croplands are diminishing and the ocean's fish stocks are in decline. These grim warning signs are matched with some positive signs of awareness in society for health, environmental stewardship and animal welfare. As a response to the problems being caused by conventional farming techniques the term sustainable food is now used to describe food production that does not take more natural resources than it gives back. Because sustainable food producers see nature as an ally rather than as an obstacle, they are able to produce more wholesome food in symbiosis with nature and the surrounding community.

Defined by the UK government Sustainable Development Commission, sustainable food is:

- Safe, healthy and nutritious, for consumers in shops, restaurants, schools, hospitals, etc. and can meet the needs of the less well-off people

- Provides a viable livelihood for farmers, processors and retailers, whose employees enjoy a safe and hygienic working environment whether in the United Kingdom or overseas

- Respects biophysical and environmental limits in its production and processing, while reducing energy consumption and improving the wider environment; it also respects the highest standards of animal health and welfare, compatible with the production of affordable food for all sectors of society

- Supports rural economies and the diversity of rural culture, in particular through an emphasis on local products that keep food miles to a minimum

The term sustainable food may not sound exciting as a description but catering businesses who develop processes to improve the sustainability of the food they offer stand a better chance of meeting the growing demands of individual consumers.

Sustainability in restaurant operations is no longer the rallying cry from a marginalized section of society. Once the domain of students and hippies the movement has moved into mainstream society and is represented by some very prominent industry players. Recently Starbucks, for example, has started selling four categories of what it calls 'sustainable coffees', and the Red Lobster chain in the United States of America, part of the Darden Environmental Trust, pledges to 'find the right balance between feeding the growing population and preserving nature'. On the Ben & Jerry's web site there are several pages describing its sustainable practices. The North American trade group, the Chefs Collaborative with over 1,000 restaurant industry members practice and encourage sustainability.

The nature of sustainable foods often means that they are more expensive to produce than other types of food. Inevitably, there is a danger that restaurant operations seeking to provide clients with sustainable food choices may increase prices. To date, there is limited evidence that individual restaurant consumers are prepared to both purchase and pay a premium for sustainable food products. Comparatively little research has been done on consumer attitudes toward sustainable food, it seems that although consumer awareness of sustainability is growing, it is not yet making a huge difference to what customers choose to buy when they shop for food, or sit down to eat in a restaurant. While the family of sustainable restaurants is wide and can include prosperous niche operations such as organic, vegetarian or healthy food eateries that send a message of health and vitality, results from studies suggest that if a restaurant is planning on 'going sustainable' and simply promoting environmental friendliness and stakeholder commitment, it might not have a striking success. How it purchases ingredients, could make sense from an environmental, moral and investor-relations perspective but it might not make much difference to customers.

The Co-Operative Group, a London-based union of retail businesses committed to socially and economically responsible business practices, recently conducted a study which revealed that while 30% of people said that they were concerned about the environmental and ethical aspects of products and services, only 3% translated those concerns into personal action. However, the green movement is rapidly spreading and it can only be a question of time before these numbers increase. A similar discrepancy was recorded by the US-based Seafood Choices Alliance, an industry trade group that promotes sustainable fishing practices. Researchers who study consumer behavior have long tried to explain the gap between what customers say and how they actually behave. In the case of guests being more or less likely to purchase foods labeled sustainable, much light has been shed by researcher Wendy Gordon, whose study 'Brand Green: Mainstream or Forever Niche?' was published in 2002 by the Green Alliance in London. Gordon argues that people tend to classify most social issues in one of two spheres: the circle of concern and the circle of influence. The latter contains problems that people feel they can control through direct action, such as what they buy. The circle of concern tends to include issues that people feel are so big that their personal actions can do little to change it – and most consumers still tend to put sustainability issues, including food, in this category.

If the term 'sustainable' is not the most appealing to customer, the philosophy behind the word appears to be a driver for restaurant businesses. Research in 2003 for the UK Institute for Grocery Distribution found that 45% of consumers would like to know more about the food they are offered when eating out-of-home. When offered meals that include organic ingredients, free range meats or fair-trade products, 52% say that they would be pleased; 45% think they would be likely to order such food. In the same year the UK Meat and Livestock Commission showed that 71% of consumers believe that the meat they are eating in the out-of-home market is British, when the reality is that supply of home-produced meat in the total foodservice market is less than 40%.

FOOD SECURITY AND GENETIC ENGINEERING

Issues of food security and genetic engineering are becoming important factors influencing consumers to turn toward sustainable foods. People are becoming increasingly concerned about the quality and safety of the food they consume. The recent food scares and the outcry over genetically modified foods have heightened consumer awareness over the quality, safety and source of foods. The US Centers for Disease Control and Prevention claims foodborne illnesses, many from fresh produce, send 300,000 Americans to the hospital every year. Foodborne pathogens are responsible for 76 million illnesses every year. The number of young people who had a food or digestive allergy increased 18% between 1997 and 2007, according to the same organization. In 2007, approximately 3 million US children and teenagers under age 18 – or nearly 4% of that age group – were reported to have a food or digestive allergy in the previous 12 months, compared to just over 2.3 million (3.3%) in 1997.

Many people see genetically modified food as a worrying technology. Advocates of genetically modified food products see them as a near-perfect solution for reducing environmental impacts, improving human health and creating new products with enhanced long-term health benefits. They argue that these higher yielding crops are urgently needed in order to deal with rising global hunger and undernourishment. Opponents argue that biotechnology interferes with the forces of evolution and could bring about unpredictable outcomes. The long-term environmental risks and impacts on human health have not been analyzed sufficiently (IFOAM, 2008). Fears also include upsetting the balance of nature, loosing biodiversity and the development of unmanageable plant characteristics. In addition, the ethical question can be asked whether humans have the right to interfere with nature on such an enormous scale.

WHICH TYPES OF FOOD CAN BE CONSIDERED FOOD?

Defining what is unsustainable or 'junk food' would be easier for most people. People are used to seeing 'organic' food in supermarkets and some have an understanding of organic food production. Similarly 'Fairtrade' food is often understood and easily spotted by its label. However, developing a label for 'sustainable' food would be a daunting task because the defining principles associated with sustainable food include environmental issues, health-related issues and social issues. The main impacts of many of the foodstuffs supplied to hotels and restaurants may have been in processing, packing or distribution, not just at the stage of producing raw materials.

Certain types of food can be identified as more sustainable (but not necessarily more healthy) than other types, for example.

Local food

It means less environmental impact resulting from travel (food miles) and buying locally helps support the local economy. The 'localvore' movement (also known as the 'hundred mile diet', where participants choose to consume only locally produced foods) is gaining momentum. However, it can be naïve to imagine that this practice is automatically more energy efficient than transported produce. Locally produced sausages can hardly be described as sustainable if the ingredients are coming from the other side of the country or continent and it could be less fresh than sea trout flown in from thousands of miles away.

Fair prices for local farmers

The immense reduction in transport costs, cheap food production in developing countries as well as the increase of big food companies and supermarket chains are responsible for dramatically reducing farm-gate prices in industrialized nations. Local shops are increasingly disappearing and effects on rural economies and farming communities are detrimental (Defra, 2007).

The Soil Association (2008) sees organic meat production in the United Kingdom in real danger unless pricing structures are reconsidered. Organic producers of beef and lamb are being paid prices that do not meet the cost of production, hence, increasing the likelihood of them reducing their organic stock or discontinuing organic production. Additionally, new regulations, forcing organic farmers to use 100% organic feed are putting even higher pressure on them. The average organic beef price in 2006 in England was £2.88 per kilo, compared to average costs of production of £3.32 per kilo (Soil Association, 2008). A significant increase in farm-gate prices seems to be the only way to ensure short- and long-term organic beef farming. Due to the distribution systems now in place, more and more money is going to supermarket chains or big food corporations instead of to the local farmers. Now in Germany, for example, only about 20% of the price of food goes to the farmer, whereas they received 75% of the share in the 1950s.

New sustainable systems of distribution need to be developed that pay local farmers a fair price reflecting the real costs of production.

Assured foods

The complexity if the issue is typified by the number of different schemes that set certain standards covering one or more of the following: food safety and traceability, animal welfare, environmental protection. The world standard GlobalGap and in Europe the EurepGAP standard are designed to help producers improve food quality and safety, biodiversity, more efficient use of natural resources, minimum use of pesticides and fertilizers and worker health and safety. A proliferation of signage is in use around the world, in the United Kingdom the red tractor sign is used. An example of another label certifying reductions in environmental impact is the label 'Stop-Climate-Change'(SCC). In Germany, these products claim to be 'climate neutral', since all carbon emissions along the complete product chain are identified, reduced and made neutral.

Organic food (see also section: Organic food, page 69)

Food labeled as organic is produced in heavily regulated agricultural systems that stipulate what can be added to crops in terms of fertilizer or pest treatment, how waste is dealt with and how animals must be reared. There are many different labels for organic food that can create confusion when consumers are not familiar with farming and production practices.

Seasonality

Restaurant menus should be based on ingredients that are in season and chefs should look for inspiration from the flow of seasons and the fresh products that become available. Seasonal offerings not only reduce the importation of food out of season i.e. food miles but also enhance local and regional diversity of plant and animal varieties as well as often leading to a rediscovery of local cooking traditions. Northern Europeans consuming strawberries in the winter months are contributing to environmental degradation. Strawberries cultivated in the south of Spain require water that is pumped from diminishing water tables.

Fairtrade food

Food coming from farmers in developing countries with the Fairtrade label receive better prices for their products and have decent working conditions. Fairtrade initiatives are often in tandem with local economic development, this sustainable approach benefits the community at large.

Historically, small farmers in developing countries who produce commodities such as coffee, cocoa, sugar or rubber are often not being paid 'fair' prices due to the consolidation of large companies and the number of intermediaries taking a share of the profit. In many situations these farmers often just provide labor and a small part of the capital expenditure but normally do not own the product. Through these contractual relationships the value of the food product is distributed up the food chain, lowering returns for farmers dramatically. 'Fairtrade' is an initiative designed to help especially small-scale farmers to survive in the global economy. Globally, the market share of fair-trade products only accounts for about 2%. Products certified with the 'Fairtrade' logo guarantee strict standards worldwide on certain environmental, labor and remuneration aspects. The Fairtrade Labelling Organization International (FLO), is an independent standard-setting body and oversees the certification process. Fair wages, fair working conditions, fair distribution of benefits, ethical business practice, respect of human rights, culture and the environment are critical elements for getting certified. The system covers food products such as bananas, cocoa, coffee, oil, seeds, rice, tea, sugar and also vegetables and fruits (FLO, 2007).

CASE STUDY 6.1: Sustainable Coffee at Scandic

Scandic is the first major Swedish hotel company to serve only 'Fairtrade' certified coffee. Every year Scandic serves 9 million cups of Fairtrade coffee at the Swedish hotels alone. Fairtrade is an ethical and social product labelling organization. Growers receive fair pay, and enabling them to send their children to school. At the Scandic hotels in Denmark, UTZ certified coffee is served. UTZ guarantees that the coffee is grown with social and environmental responsibility, and the coffee can always be traced to a country and grower. 'When you drink a cup of coffee at Scandic, you are helping to ensure a better life for the growers and their families' is a clear statement to the customers.

Source: http://www.scandichotels.com/About-Us/Responsible-living/Society/

NUTRITION AND HEALTH

It would be foolish to claim that eating large daily portions of sustainably produced pork, cheesecake and cream would be healthy. However, the concept of sustainable lifestyles is closely associated with purchasing sustainable food. The choice of food and the way it is produced and manufactured, has a significant impact on the health of individuals. Good nutrition and good sustainable food products are the best way to good health. While many people in the western world eat well a large number do not, particularly among the more disadvantaged and vulnerable in society. In particular, a significant proportion of the population consume less than the recommended amount of fruit and vegetables and fiber but more than the recommended amount of fat, saturated fat, salt and sugar. Such poor nutrition is a major cause of ill health and premature death.

Cancer and cardiovascular disease, including heart disease and stroke are the major causes of death. About one third of cancers can be attributed to poor diet and nutrition. Unhealthy diets, along with physical inactivity, have also contributed to the growth of obesity. In England, 22% of men and 23% of women are now obese, a trebling since the 1980s, and 65% of men and 56% of women – 24 million adults – are either overweight or obese. It is a growing problem with children and young people too. Around 16% of 2 to 15 year olds are now obese (Defra, 2007). Obesity brings its own health problems, including hypertension, heart disease and type 2 diabetes. Obesity is responsible for an estimated 9,000 premature deaths per year in England. It is estimated that the treatment of ill health from poor diet costs the National Health Service (NHS) at least £4 billion each year (Defra, 2007).

Cooking methods

Food preparation has great influence on diets, health and diet-related diseases such as obesity. In order to ensure healthy food that tastes great, it is important to choose correct cooking methods. Preparation techniques should always maintain maximum nutrient retention. Exposing foods to light or air, cooking on high temperatures, using too much liquid or cooking for long periods may reduce nutrient levels. Traditional cooking methods are well suited to healthy cooking. Pan frying and deep-frying should be avoided as well as the tendency of adding too much butter, cream and salt.

Food production issues

The main preoccupation of the food economy is to increase production in order to feed the growing world population and fulfill the culinary desires of the developed nations. Unfortunately, issues such as the quality of products, nutritional value and health implications are sometimes neglected. Recent problems, much reported by the media include health scares such as BSE; health problems such as heart disease and obesity due to inadequate diets; over-consumption in developed countries and under-nutrition in developing countries; ecological disasters such as over-fishing and intensive factory farming of animals. A sustainable food and beverage model requires the whole food supply chain, from food production to food sourcing to food preparation needs to be respectful of both human health and the environment.

Monocultures and the loss of biodiversity

In most parts of the world, food supply has moved from local, small-scale production to highly concentrated production and mass distribution of food-stuffs. As a result of the increase in industrial monoculture significant crop and livestock diversity has been lost. In the nineteenth century 80–90% of vegetable and fruit varieties that were common had been lost by the end of the twentieth century. For example, of the 7,098 apple varieties documented as having been eaten between 1804 and 1904 in the United States of America, approximately 86% have been lost. Biodiversity is immensely important for the environment, its loss leads to environmental degradation and significantly reduces the natural defense systems of the earth in the face of climate change, natural disasters and the interference of humankind and other changes. Dr. Vandana Shiva, India's most famous combatant for the preservation of biodiversity and opponent of globalization, stresses the importance of bio-diversity for human health, quality and taste of food products as well as for preserving our ecosystems. She maintains that monocultures are not sustain-able and their lack of resistance to climatic change is too high. In addition to endangering biodiversity, monocultures increase unsustainable energy usage by reducing human labor and placing energy focus on machinery.

Organic food

More and more people are buying organically grown fresh foods, so much so, that in the United Kingdom demand seriously outstrips supply. Currently 70% of the organic produce sold in the United Kingdom is imported. The same situation exists with organic vegetable boxes where 40% of the produce supplied in the boxes is imported from Continental Europe. Organic food sales increased between 17% and 21% in the United States each year since 1997 compared with other food sales which have been growing at an aver-age rate of 2–4% a year (Organic Trade Association, 2007). Similar growth has been seen in other Western economies. The Organic Trade Association estimates that current sales of organic products in the United States total $15 billion. This rapid growth makes it an attractive market for mainstream food companies that are looking for new ways to grow their businesses. Organic food has permeated the global food marketing chain provoking intense responses from sympathetic critics that organic farming's authen-ticity is being threatened as it scales up operations to meet the demands of mass marketing.

It is emphasized that organic farming is a socially caring system of agriculture that aims to produce healthy food while preserving the natural environment. Organic farming contributes significantly in the protection of the ecosystem, the biodiversity, the drinking water and the earth itself. Organic food production does not permit the use of synthetic fertilizers, pesticides and growth regulators. Genetically modified plant stock, food irradiation as well as food additives are prohibited. Organic livestock has to be fed on recognized organic feed. The overall concept of organic farming is based on a closed-loop production that includes animal husbandry, pest management, soil fertility and the abandonment of genetic engineering and nitrogen fertilizer. Furthermore, it is necessary that the agricultural crop land has a rotation of different crops including fruit and forage crops. Vegetable fiber and dung are returned to the soil. If a farm does not keep animals, the crop rotation has to include a considerable amount of nitrogen rich plants as substitutes. All animals have to be kept in humane conditions.

According to the Soil Association (2008) organic farming results in multiple environmental benefits such as a higher level of biodiversity, a lower pollution from pesticides, lower energy use and carbon emissions and a lower level of waste. Various social and economic benefits are derived from organic farming as well. Increase consumers' interest in farming, contribution to rural employment and high standard of animal welfare are a few examples of those benefits. Due to higher production costs, organic food is comparatively more expensive than conventional food. Prices for organic food tend to be highest in specialist grocery stores. New forms of purchasing patterns are now developing that are effectively bringing down prices. In many countries, consumers can either buy directly from organic farms or visit farmers' markets.

Organic food and nutrients

According to the 2007 annual report of the Worldwatch Institute, today's grain, fruit and vegetables produce 10–25% less nutrients than some 50 years ago. Hence, in order to address worldwide health problems, it is of great importance to improve the nutritional quality of food. Nutrient deficient foods together with poor food choices can best explain the epidemic of obesity and diabetes that affects the western world. Conventional farming methods that increase yields by utilizing chemical fertilizers and pesticides are most responsible for this high nutrient loss, and some reports claim that organic food products contain higher concentrations of valuable nutrients.

Dr. Maria Amodio and Dr. Adel Kader from the University of California published research in the *Journal of the Science of Food and Agriculture* in 2007 that convincingly showed that some organic food is better. They found that 'all the main mineral constituents were more concentrated in their sample of organic kiwi fruit which also had 14% more ascorbic acid (vitamin C) and a higher polyphenol content, an antioxidant useful in the fight against cancer'. They also observed organic fruit to have thicker skins which, they suggest, may have developed as a natural defense mechanism against pests in the absence of chemicals to kill them. However, there are conflicting views concerning the health benefits of organic food. In recent years, criticism of organic food flared across national and international media. Some targeted the perceived nutritional value of organic food, others the power of organic agriculture for sustainable development. Finally, others questioned potential effects of organic food trade on food miles or its global scale production possibilities.

Scientists agree that organic food products contain lower value of toxins, nitrates and pesticides. The value of vitamins and minerals is the same or even higher. However, the nutritional value depends on the plant, the location, the season, the weather, the animal, the gender, the age and several other aspects. Research conducted to date has not produced a final conclusion about the taste of organic food products; there is no overwhelming evidence that organic food tastes better. Regardless, many consumers perceive organic food to taste better.

CASE STUDY 6.2: Demeter

The world largest association of marketers offering ecological wares. It is a brand for biodynamic products and procedures focusing on the long-term sustainability of agriculture. As an international brand, Demeter is represented in 38 countries worldwide, and their working procedures are implemented by 3200 farms. Each year Demeter-products have a sales volume of about €220 million. Only approved partners, who are strictly controlled and contractually bounded, are allowed to use the brand name.

There is a continuous control mechanism, beginning with the cultivation and ending with the distribution. Through every single step the Demeter partners have to fulfil the production and process standards of the organisation. In addition to opposing the use of synthetic fertilizers and pesticides, the Demeter organisation focuses on the protection of natural resources. 'Demeter farmers and procedures actively contribute towards the shaping of a future worth living for and creating healthy foods with distinctive taste' 'Foods with Character' – Demeter – 'the Brand you can trust." (Demeter publicity quote). The Demeter product range also includes natural cosmetics and textile products from wool and cotton.

Source: Demeter-International: http://www.demeter.net/

ORGANIC LABELING

Various voluntary certification programs and standards for organic agriculture have been developed in the last 20 years. In addition to numerous private organic standards worldwide, more than 60 governments have already codified organic standards into technical regulations (IFOAM, 2008). In the United States, the US Department of Agriculture has established a set of national standards for any food handling organization that wants to sell organically produced foods (USDA, 2006). In the European Union, all organic products must be certified by an approved organization such as The Soil Association based in the United Kingdom, Sweden's KRAV or Australian Certified Organic. The aim of these national standards is to assure consumers that 'the organic foods they purchase are produced, processed and certified to be consistent with national organic standards' (USDA, 2007).

Under European Union Eco-regulation, products certified under organic certification schemes, cannot be labeled as 'organic' if they contain genetically modified plant cells. Food labeled as '100 percent organic' must contain only organically produced ingredients. Food labeled 'organic' has to contain a minimum of 95% organically produced ingredients. If labeled to be 'made with organic ingredients' the food must contain at least 70% organic ingredients.

CASE STUDY 6.3: Bio Seal in German Gastronomy and Hospitality

Since 2003, restaurants and other retailers can label food products, dishes or whole menus on their menu with the bio seal. In order to get this organic certification, they need to take part in the control procedure of the 'EG-Öko-Verordnung'. All levels of production and processing of the food products as well as their final preparation in the kitchen are controlled. If a whole dish is labeled with the bio seal, at least 95 percent of the ingredients have to be organically produced. Control in restaurant kitchens becomes very complicated as the origin of all the ingredients used in a recipe have to be identified. Depending on the size of the restaurants, a price of between €150 and €600 has to be paid to obtain the organic certification for one year.

Source: Dehoga: http://www.dehoga-bundesverband.de

FOOD MILES

In the 21st century, the food westerners eat generally does not follow seasonal rhythms and can be characterized as coming from nowhere in particular. The food industry has been significantly affected by globalization and modern supply chain management practices and capabilities. Consumers buy foods that are grown or produced far away from the consumption location.

The 'food miles' or, more accurately, the 'food transportation' debate is concerned with the environmental and social costs associated with food transport, from where it is produced to where it is processed, to the wholesaler, to the retailer or catering outlet and to the consumer (Defra). Defra identified the major cultural, structural and commercial reasons for the increase in food miles as coming from:

- An increase in consumption of food that cannot be grown in the country, for example, oranges for juicing.

- Consumer demand for year-round food resulting in importation of out-of-season produce.

- Lower prices of imported food products.

- Increases in leisure travel and consequent exposure to and demand for exotic food products.

- Growth of out-of-town shopping centers and the resulting increase in traveling by shoppers.

- Growth of prepared and processed foods leading to the centralization of processing and, consequently, increases in travel to and from factories and processing centers.

- Simplified procurement processes, reduction of a supplier base, and a resulting tendency not to purchase from small-scale local producers.

- Changes in consumer lifestyle and demographics leading to an increase in preference for readymade food and food consumed outside the home.

- Growth in numbers of logistics service providers and their tendency to offer an ever increasing range of services.

The interest in food miles is based on its effects on the environment, sustainable agricultural development, local food systems and socio-economic development.

Food miles are significant and growing in number. They accounted for 33 billion vehicle kilometers globally in 2002 and they gave rise to around 20 million tons of CO_2. Air freight of food accounts for only 0.1% of the vehicle kilometers. However, air freight accounts for 10% of the food miles CO_2 equivalent emissions (Defra, 2006). The external costs of food miles are high in terms of greenhouse gas emissions, air pollution, noise, congestion, accidents. The necessary infrastructure in the United Kingdom associated with food miles are estimated at just over £9 billion pounds each year.

Importing organic Argentinian beef to Europe leads to about eight times the transport emissions compared to a similar joint of Welsh beef, being sold in south-east England. When consumers want to be environmentally friendly, it is not necessarily the best solution to purchase imported organic produce from far away. The proximity of the food plays an important aspect as well. Additionally, fresh food products start to loose their nutritional content in storage: as time increases between harvesting and consumption, the nutrient value decreases. For example spinach, if kept at room temperature loses between 50% and 80% of its vitamin C content within 24 hours.

According to some more critical sources, the concept of food miles in regards to sustainability is not as simple in reality. As argued in the study 'The Validity of Food Miles as an Indicator for Sustainable Development' conducted by Defra (2006), a 'single indicator based on total food kilometers is an inadequate indicator of sustainability'. Differences in food production systems need to be taken into consideration, for example. If imported food has been produced more sustainably than local food, the impact of food transport can be offset to some extent. Hence, it could be more energy efficient to import tomatoes from Spain than producing them in heated greenhouses near the end consumer. As the amount of greenhouse emissions also depend on factors such as the transport mode or transport efficiency, further research into these issues is necessary. Socio-economic issues have to be taken into consideration as well. Since the subject is high on the public agenda, restaurants pursuing a policy of sustainability should source organic food that is produced as close to the point of consumption as possible.

CASE STUDY 6.4: The Real Bath Breakfast in the United Kingdom

Run by Friends of the Earth as part of their 'Real Food Campaign', the aim of 'The Real Bath Breakfast' was to promote the use of locally produced, GM-free, organic foods, produced without the use of pesticides. Those hotels or guesthouses that want to be marked out by 'The Real Bath Breakfast' need to use ingredients that have been, if possible, produced within a 40-mile radius of Bath Abbey. Coffee and tea served at the breakfast should be purchased as 'fair-trade' products. The aim is to support local businesses and hence the local economy. Reducing food miles as well as packaging waste should benefit the environment. Furthermore, real fresh produce, containing fewer chemicals than mass-produced products, aims to enhance human health.

Source: BathTourismPlus (2008), http://www.bathnes.gov.uk

CASE STUDY 6.5: Xanterra Parks & Resorts

The American national park concessionaire Xanterra Parks & Resorts operates successfully a sustainable cuisine program that encompasses most of their 64 restaurants. In 2001 they started off with banning four types of fish from their menu: Chilean Sea Bass, Atlantic Swordfish, Blue Fin Tuna and Shark. They are threatened by over-fishing, or harvested in ways that damage the environment. Today Xanterra Parks & Resorts serves seafood certified by the Marine Stewardship Council (MSC) and thus adhering to guidelines developed by Monterey Bay Aquarium Seafood Watch protocol and the Audubon Society's Living Oceans Seafood Guide. They were the first foodservice chain in the US to pursue the MSC 'chain of custody' certification, which provides traceability of their seafood back to the source. These sources not only provide wild Alaskan Salmon, fished in a sustainable manner, but also farm-raised trout, shrimp and abalone. Examples of menu items include a pinwheel of wild Alaskan salmon with sautéed spinach and organic red lentil at the Lake Yellowstone Hotel Dining Room and Kal-bi style teriyaki chicken made with free-range chicken from Fulton Valley farms at the Silverado Resort in Napa Valley.

Not only do the restaurants serve such sustainable cuisine menus, Xanterra Parks & Resorts employees enjoy organic food at some of their dining operations as well as guests of some catering events. Besides seafood the menu offerings have grown significantly, including the addition of Oregon Country Natural Beef, Kuobuta Pork, Kobe-style Beef, local dairy, wines produced using sustainable practices, and hormone- and antibiotic-free elk, bison and venison. Furthermore they have stepped into a partnership with Green Mountain Coffee Roasters, Inc., who promotes Fair Trade Certified coffee. The growth and harvest of organic coffee beans is completed in a sustainable manner, cutting out the use of pesticides and working a 'shade-growing' method, protecting the rainforest and its natural inhabitants. The beans are purchased from local farmers at a fair price.

Source: Xanterra Parks & Resorts: http://www.xanterra.com

SOURCING WINE

Currently, there are several recognized sustainable schemes for wines available, such as Agriculture Raisonnée in France, Sustainable Winegrowing in New Zealand, Integrated Production of Wine in South Africa and the California Integrated Winemaking Alliance. Sustainable Winegrowing New Zealand, for example, aims to help companies to work toward improving performance in regard to environmental, social and economic sustainability in the vineyards (Sustainable Winegrowing New Zealand, 2008). Some of these organizations are independently audited, others are self-audited and each of the schemes has different criteria for judging and giving accreditation.

Wines deemed to be sustainable normally fall into three categories; organic, biodynamic and vegan wines.

Organic wines

As wine is extremely fragile by nature, winemakers have added sulfites for centuries. However, wine carrying an 'organic' label must be made from

100% certified organic grapes, without any added sulfites. Around 200 different chemicals have been found in conventionally produced wines. Without the use of chemical fertilizers, herbicides or insecticides a healthy and biologically active soil can be maintained for growing grapes. Instead of applying herbicides in the vineyard, the soil is cultivated and cover crops are planted. Natural fertilizer, such as composted animal manure is used and biodiversity of plants is promoted in order to naturally regulate the vineyard soil. Because more manual operations are involved, organic wines are normally more expensive than conventional ones. There is no doubt that organic wine is better for the environment and the people that work in the vineyards are protected from effects of chemicals.

There is a distinction between wine labeled 'produced from organically grown grapes' and wine simply labeled 'organic'. In contrast to the latter, wine labeled as 'produced from organically grown grapes' is allowed to contain up to 100 ppm of added sulfites per liter (Organic Wine Company, 2007).

Biodynamic

Biodynamic farmers also focus on establishing a healthy soil but take the organic approach a step further. They use homeopathic sprays, herbal preparations and the lunar cycles in order to increase soil fertility and protect vines from pests and diseases (Organic Vintners, 2002). The Organic Wine Company (2007) describes this method of agriculture as 'ultra-organic' and states that it was developed at the beginning of this century, based on theories of the social philosopher Rudolf Steiner. Biodynamic farmers plant their crops according to the belief that plant development is a flow of chemical energy that radiates from the moon, stars and the planets.

Vegan wines

Both organic and conventional winemakers frequently use animal products during the clarification and fining process. These animal products include egg white to brighten red wine, milk proteins to make wine taste softer and gelatin to remove bitterness. A wine classified as a 'vegan wine', on the other hand, does not use any animal-derived products.

CHAPTER QUESTIONS

1. How would you describe sustainable food?
2. What types of food can be considered sustainable?
3. Describe some common health problems that can result from poor eating habits.
4. What is organic agricultural production?

5. What is understood by the term 'food miles'?

6. Describe three types of sustainable wine.

READING LIST

Amodio, M.L., Colelli, G., Hasey, J.K., Kader., Adel, A.A., 2007. A comparative study of composition and postharvest performance of organically and conventionally grown. Journal of the Science of Food and Agriculture 87 (7), 1228–1236, © Society of Chemical Industry, reproduced with permission of John Wiley & Sons Ltd on behalf of the SCI.

Chef Collaborative: http://www.chefscollaborative.org/

The Co-Operative: http://www.co-operative.coop/

Darden Environmental Trust: http://www.dardenusa.com/com_ff_preservation.asp

Department for Environment, Food and Rural Affairs (Defra): http://www.defra.gov.uk

Global Partnership for Safe and Sustainable Agriculture (EUREGAP): http://www.eurepgap.org/

Fairtrade Labelling Organizations International (FLO) http://www.fairtrade.net

Food Standard Agency (FSA): http://www.food.gov.uk

The Global Partnership for Good Agricultural Practice (GLOBALGAP): http://www.globalgap.org/

Gordon, W., 2002. Brand Green; Mainstream Or Forever Niche? SOS Free Stock, UK.

The Institute of Grocery Distribution (IGD): http://www.igd.com/index.asp?id=0

International Foundation for Organic Agriculture Movements (IFOAM) (2008). Organic standards and certification. Available from http://www.ifoam.org/about_ifoam/standards/index.html

National Health Service (NHS): http://www.nhs.uk/

Organic Trade Association (OTA): http://www.ota.com/organic

Organic Wine Company: http://www.theorganicwinecompany.com

Seafood Choices Alliance: http://www.seafoodchoices.com/home.php

Shiva, V., 2000. Stolen Harvest: The Hijacking of the Global Food Supply. South End Press, Cambridge, MA.

Soil Association, 2008. Organic food and farming report. Soil Association, Bristol.

Sustainable Development Commission UK (SDC): http://www.sd-commission.org.uk/

Sustainable Wine Growing New Zealand: http://www.nzwine.com

United States Department of Agriculture (USDA) (2008): http://www.usda.gov/wps/portal/usdahome

US Center for Disease Control and Prevention (CDC): http://www.cdc.gov/

Worldwatch Institute: http://www.worldwatch.org/

CHAPTER 7

Energy Efficient Kitchens

Study Objectives

- To explain how much energy is often wasted in kitchens
- To describe energy efficient practice
- To describe new energy efficient kitchen equipment technology

KITCHENS: PROBLEM DEFINITION

Kitchens are by far the most energy intensive sector of any hospitality operation. In the United States, according to Pacific Gas and Electric Company 80% of the $10 billion annual energy bill for the commercial food service sector is spent on inefficient food cooking, holding and storage equipment. According to the UK Green Hotelier magazine, kitchen energy consumption can be reduced by up to one third, through measures such as using energy-efficient equipment and encouraging efficient staff practices. With careful planning and organization these savings can be made without sacrificing service, quality, style or comfort while making significant contributions to a cleaner environment at the same time.

A restaurant kitchen cost analysis carried out by The US Green Restaurant Association revealed the following energy usage break down:

• Food preparation (cooking appliances)	22%
• Sanitation	18%
• HVAC (heating, ventilation and air conditioning)	17%
• Lighting	13%
• Kitchen exhaust systems and ventilation	11%
• Refrigeration	6%
• Miscellaneous (maintenance, cleaning, etc.)	13%

The main areas where energy is used in kitchens include cooking (food preparation and food service equipment); hot water provision; chilling, freezing and ice making; ventilation and filtration; dish washing and lighting. Technology is one way of realizing energy savings but it is not enough just to look out for eco-certified equipment.

ENERGY SAVING AND STAFF TRAINING

Energy saving in the kitchen requires long-term planning which normally starts with a kitchen energy audit performed by a trained professional. Once the areas of potential energy savings have been identified energy-efficiency upgrades can be decided upon depending on budgets and payback periods integrating energy savings can be calculated. All energy saving initiatives will include training staff and setting up clear energy saving procedures that include consumption-reduction goals. Examples of good, energy efficient kitchen practice are:

- *Operate equipment properly*. Combi ovens are a good example, only add water when necessary, extra energy is used in heating the oven when water is added. Use large pans and ovens to cook large quantities and small pans and ovens to cook small quantities otherwise extra energy is used heating the equipment and not the food. Incidentally, unnecessarily overheated kitchens are not efficient places to work and potentially force restaurant owners to spend more on cooling the air. The scorching heat required from broilers requires a great deal of energy, perhaps more than any other appliance in the kitchen. They also rank amongst the least efficient appliances in the kitchen and need to be used wisely. Consider using a heat gun for high-heat broiling, which eliminates the need to have a salamander broiler constantly running during food preparation times.

- *Turn off equipment when not in use*. The days of lighting up the cooking range when the breakfast chefs come in and not turning anything off till the last guest leaves are finished. Even leaving machinery on standby consumes energy, turn everything off when · not in use and make sure that only the necessary equipment is turned on and nothing else.

- *Cook creatively*. Cooking at lower temperatures saves energy when done wisely. Sometimes flambé work is necessary but the heat from flames should ideally always be captured. Ovens tend to be more efficient than rotisseries; griddles tend to be more efficient than broilers. Roasting at lower temperatures can be more energy efficient. In addition, cooking at lower temperatures causes less shrinkage and hence loss of nutrients. Batch cookery consumes less energy than individual portions. Pressure cooking is more efficient than shallow frying. Quality should not be sacrificed but a close examination of cooking methods might reveal potential economies.

- *Maintain and repair*. Clogged ventilation filters, oven doors that do not close properly and leaking gaskets all waste energy. Over a period of time the switches, buttons and thermostats on equipment might well become defective resulting in cooking at the wrong temperatures. Periodic recalibration is necessary to ensure this does not occur. Adjust flames on older gas oven pilot lights that are burning too high.

Correct energy conscious working practice is essential in the kitchen but making the right decisions when replacing equipment or when constructing a new kitchen is equally as critical. Often it is not cost-effective simply to replace a working piece of equipment based on energy efficiency alone, although inefficient appliances make for higher operating costs and tend to emit more heat than their efficient counterparts resulting in hotter kitchens. An evaluation must first be made of food production needs and appliances should be bought that match the output of the establishment. Grossly oversized appliances make both capital costs and operating costs higher. A good way for operators to select energy-efficient equipment is to look for a known low-energy usage certifier such as the US Energy Star qualified equipment. Energy Star certify that savings as much as 50% of energy or resources can be made on the equipment they recommend such as steam cookers (compartment steamers), commercial fryers (open pot), solid, door-type refrigeration, hot food holding cabinets, under counter, door and conveyor dish machines and cube-type ice machines. In the United States, a growing number of states and municipalities are offering rebates through utility companies to operators who purchase Energy Star certified equipment.

NEW GENERATION ENERGY EFFICIENT KITCHEN EQUIPMENT

Induction cooking equipment

Induction is generally more energy efficient than gas or conventional electric heat. These units use a power supply to generate a magnetic field around a coil located under the ceramic top of the unit. When an iron or magnetic metal pan is placed in the magnetic field, currents are induced in the cooking utensil and instant heat is generated due to resistance of the pan. Heating is instantaneous and can be regulated by output control buttons. In addition to being very fast, induction units are also very efficient as nearly all of the electrical energy consumed is converted to heat in the pan. Almost no energy is consumed when nothing is cooking. Since almost all the power consumed goes directly into the pan and not into the surrounding area, air-conditioning and hood exhaust requirements are often less than when using conventional cooking sources.

High speed ovens

Use multiple heating methods in the same piece of equipment and improved or new forms of cooking technology. They combine the best features of the convection oven, microwave oven and impingement oven to create some of the fastest quality food producing units ever introduced. Hybrid varieties exist for this type of technology. One popular style made by several companies, uses forced air in a manner similar to that of an impingement oven and augments this with microwaves. Super heated air is forced over the food to brown the outside for taste and appearance. At the same time microwave energy penetrates the food and heats it through before the circulated air can penetrate. Another hybrid oven also uses microwaves but combines this approach with high-intensity light wave energy. Others use infrared radiant heat in addition to other heating sources. Each of these approaches offers extremely fast cooking times. For the truly ecologically minded restaurateur, portable solar ovens will provide an interesting focal point for guests on the restaurant terrace during sunny days but remember to cut back on those hugely un-ecological gas fired patio heaters!

Steamers

Until recently, steamers consumed excessive amounts of water and energy. New steamers operate as a closed system without a boiler and a drain so they consume far less water and far less energy. Many of the connectionless steamers are designed with output in mind and they can produce just as much food as traditional boiler-based steamers but at a much lower cost to operate.

Deep fryers

Historically gas fryers have not been very efficient. In a typical design, gas is ignited in tubes running through or around the frying vat, and this allows much of the heat to escape directly up the flue. New designs impart much more of the heat to the cooking medium. The new generation of electric fryers are typically far more efficient since the heating element is submerged directly in the frying medium, with very high electricity to heat conversion and heat transfer. Manufacturers are also providing better insulation around the fry vats to retain more heat.

Kitchen ventilation

Many older style exhaust hoods are big-time energy consumers because they suck up a lot of the air that has already been cooled in kitchen air-conditioning systems. New, super efficient exhaust hoods and ventilators have highly efficiency filters or engineered designs to take advantage of the flow of thermal air currents to keep the amount of air wasted to a minimum. This technology is not cheap and it is more cost-effective when heavy-duty appliances (e.g. broilers, wok ranges, salamanders) are grouped together under one ventilation hood. It is worth considering placing the broiler under a separate exhaust hood with a higher exhaust rate.

LIGHTING

Some operators believe expensive equipment is much more important than making small changes. Sometimes a small investment can make big savings. Switching to CFL light bulbs has been one of the most widely embraced actions to reduce energy costs by both businesses and individuals. Changing 20 traditional 60-watt incandescent bulbs with CFL bulbs costs initially about €100, within a year around €500 euros will be saved in most countries. Turn off lights whenever possible and install occupancy sensors which automatically shut off lights when no activity is detected in storage rooms, break rooms, toilets and even walk-in refrigerators. Use light-emitting diodes (LEDs) that are a good alternative to incandescent bulbs for signage. Electricity savings can sometimes exceed 80%.

CHAPTER QUESTIONS

1. How is energy often wasted in kitchens?
2. Describe energy efficient kitchen practice.
3. Describe some examples of energy efficient kitchen equipment.

ONLINE READING LIST

Green Hotelier: http://www.greenhotelier.org/

Green Restaurant Association: http://www.dinegreen.com/

Pacific Gas and Electric Company (PG&E): http://www.pge.com/

US Energy Star: http://www.energystar.gov/

CHAPTER 8

Responsible Marketing for Hotels and Restaurants

Study Objectives

- To define sustainable marketing
- To identify the principles of responsible marketing for hotels and restaurants
- To provide an understanding of the importance of openness, honesty and credibility in the responsible marketing context
- To examine the concept of sustainable development in relation to external communications and responsible marketing
- To analyze responsible marketing within the context of a company's ethical strategy
- To appreciate the shift toward the four new 'P's of marketing

Consumers feel the impact of marketing in different ways. In some cases, a business marketing objective may be to serve the greater good of society through social marketing efforts. In other instances, a marketer's activities are open to criticism for being guilty of glamorizing consumption. Producing goods and services uses up resources, which generate waste and pollution. Hospitality operations sustain their business level by ensuring a constant flow of customers through the doors. The focus of marketing efforts is then directed at attracting more customers, enabled through the conventional marketing theory views. The traditional marketing mix with the four Ps, being product, price, place and promotion, conventionally played a leading role in influencing customers' purchasing decisions. The emphasis on satisfying customers beyond the four Ps and managing the customer experience play an increasingly central role in the marketing effort. Customers have progressed from being simple buyers, to being information technology assisted informed buyers. In most cases, businesses that undertake strict environmental protection conduct or actively support community social activities will want to communicate to customers about its engagement. Marketers influence, communicate and shape culture. They are in the position to modify consumer behavior, global environmental impacts and the financial bottom line. In practice, it is about assessing and minimizing the impacts of products and services. Through ethical promotion, publicity and branding techniques, hospitality operations can develop a customer base built on quality and trust. Customers are influenced by the four new 'P's of sustainable development: people, planet, profit and progress.

The concept of sustainable development has entered the agenda of most governments around the globe. Citizens of many nations have adapted certain modes of consumption coherent with sustainable development. Some companies have in turn adapted their marketing strategies to capture this new consumer.

CAUSE-RELATED MARKETING

Cause-related marketing appeared in the United States in the middle of 1980s where the wish to combine the sale of a product to a particular cause would lead to increased revenue streams and public recognition. The multiplication of such initiatives led some companies to making cause-related marketing a central element of their strategy. The payment of a fraction of the sales price of a product or a service to a charity organization has become a marginal element of cause-related marketing over the years. The implication of a company in a good cause now takes on several forms. It often consists of a combination of monetary gifts, premiums for voluntary employee activities or gifts in forms of equipment, products or services. Certain companies may engage in strategic partnerships with environmental charity organizations or social welfare associations. The cause-related marketing is closely linked to emotional branding, which aims at creating an emotional bond between the customer and the brand. One of the major criticisms of cause-related marketing strategy is that all marketing activities, even if attached to a particular cause, are aimed at straight consumption and tend to be narrowed in focus.

GREEN MARKETING

The principal ingredient of green marketing is not to incite consumers to consume less but to consume better. Marketing is a crucial aspect of daily business operations and can contribute to sustainable development. It is often perceived as the engine to the modes of consumption in society. It is also undoubtedly one of the best ways to change spending patterns and redefine quality standards. A growing number of marketing professionals and companies are enthusiastic about reinventing marketing starting with the ethical responsibilities with one particular goal in sight: to encourage responsible consumption.

There is a fundamental dilemma between the dual objectives of green marketing: stimulating consumption to generate profit and the desire to regulate the fluctuation of modern day modes of consumption. Economic profitability should therefore be perceived as not an end in itself but as a means to sustainable development. Green marketing requires a reconsideration of traditional marketing principles in the following areas:

- Initial positioning of the company within a market
- Image perceived by the customers
- The legitimacy of environmental positioning for the company
- The acceptability of green products and services by customers
- Customer expectations
- The customer's perception of the benefits that a green product or service offers

CHARACTERISTICS OF GREEN MARKETING

Consideration of Future Generations

Considering the needs of future generations when providing products and services in the present.

Businesses are responsible in the same level as individuals

Maintaining a durable positive image of the company in relation to environmental protection. Companies that communicate respect for the environment and the protection of natural resources, demonstrate a human approach to business. This principle reflects the neoclassical theory that nature is the *captial* whereby resources are converted into finished goods. The neoclassicists never considered nature to be an inexhaustible reserve of resources, today modern man consumes many times over what the planet can offer.

Ethical responsibility of businesses

Green marketing is about the creation of a bridge between businesses and all stakeholders based on ethical behavior, by embarking on a process of cooperation. The common code of ethics is based on the fact that a generation is entitled to a quality of life at least as good as the preceding one.

Green marketing is a holistic approach that endeavors to demonstrate that companies are not solely interested in their profit but in the well-being of the planet and its inhabitants.

Sustainable marketing: a definition

Marketing has a tremendous influence on the environmental and social impacts of businesses and their products, policies and production processes. Marketers play an important part in developing a corporate strategy. The boundaries between 'corporate' and 'marketing' strategies are often blurred. Marketers are then well placed to exert a positive influence in helping businesses to become sustainable. Sustainable marketing utilizes the traditional marketing methods to understand the values, emotions and the buying behavior of potential customers with the goal of establishing a sustainable, restorative relationship. Sustainable marketing can be defined as the establishment, maintenance and enhancement of customer relationships in order that the objectives of the parties involved are met without compromising the ability of future generations to achieve their own objectives. Consequently, rather than being a simple extension to traditional marketing, sustainable marketing represents a discontinuous shift in corporate philosophy. It is a holistic approach to marketing where the impacts of all activities, from cradle to grave, are considered. Responsibility is a keyword in sustainable marketing. Sustainable marketing is simply defined as *Responsible Marketing*, where 'responsible' is the contribution that the marketing profession can make to sustainable development.

THE MARKETING ENVIRONMENT REVISITED

While a detailed explanation of marketing analysis is beyond the scope of this chapter, an important aspect is the marketing environment which comprises all actors and issues that affect marketing decisions and practices of a business (Kotler). The marketing environment is split into two. The micro-environment in which customers, competitors, suppliers and distributors influence the way a business performs its day-to-day tasks. The other being the macro-environment that includes broader influences, such as politics, economics, technology and social trends that usually have long-term and irregular impacts on a business.

There are two additional aspects of the conventional macro-environmental analysis that are missing. Firstly the *physical environment* is not considered as part of the marketing environment even though the planet ultimately underpins all that a business achieves. Secondly the analysis of the marketing environment is set in the present time with the sole consideration of today's generation of customers, shareholders, employees and other stakeholders.

THE MARKETING P'S REVISITED

The sustainable development paradigm, founded on the three axes of social equity, environment and economy, provide the underlying bases for re-defining the traditional four Ps of marketing (product, price, place and promotion). Hence the three Ps of sustainable marketing become people, planet and profit, as depicted in Figure 8.1.

In addition, the fourth P for progress becomes a logical extension. Progress is the driver by which businesses integrate ethics and long-term commitment to a better world order within the company mission statement (see Figure 8.2).

Businesses do not operate in bubbles. The activities of competitors, suppliers, distributors and consumers all play a role in the potential impact a company can have – may it be environmental, social or economical. A

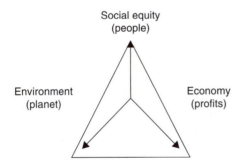

Sustainable development is often represented as a triangle in order to emphasize the three following objectives:

1. Economy (The creation of wealth for all financial participants through modes of production and consumption which are sustainable).

2. Environment (The conservation and the management of natural resources).

3. Social Equity (The benefit streams for all people directly involved and society at large).

One particular objective should not be achieved to the detriment of the two others. The goal is for the three objectives to be attained simultaneously.

FIGURE 8.1 *The new three Ps in relation to the pillars of sustainability.*

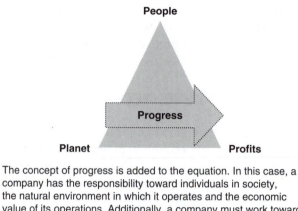

The concept of progress is added to the equation. In this case, a
company has the responsibility toward individuals in society,
the natural environment in which it operates and the economic
value of its operations. Additionally, a company must work towards
continuous improvements and progress in the creation of a better
world.

FIGURE 8.2 *The new four P's of Sustainable Marketing.*

company cannot operate in a vacuum looking at its own products, services
and processes individually. The development of product and services must
be assumed within the broader perspective of societal welfare. To sum up,
responsible marketing is the common denominator in this business strategy.

LIFE-CYCLE ASSESSMENT

A life-cycle assessment (LCA) – also known as life-cycle analysis, ecobal-
ance and cradle-to-grave analysis – is the investigation and evaluation of
environmental impacts of a given product or service caused or necessitated
by its existence. The goal of LCA is to compare the full range of environmental damage assignable to products and services and to be able to choose
the least burdensome one. LCA offers clear links to marketing functions.
In addition, societal impacts are measured by a similar process known as
Societal Impact Analysis (SIA).

Hospitality businesses are encouraged to look at the whole *life cycle* of
their products. Life cycle analysis is the measurement of:

- The extraction and transportation of raw material to the production site
- The use of all water and energy and additional material used in the
  manufacturing process
- The impacts caused during the distribution including all intervening
  transportation
- The impacts engendered during usage and disposal

The sum of all those steps or phases is the *life cycle* of the product. Food cultivation cumulated transport impacts, distribution activities, preparation and waste disposal, all add up to the life cycle carbon footprint of a typical hospitality food product. Thus, hospitality managers are provided with a clear insight into where financial and non-financial costs lay.

The food sector is often considered as one of the most resource-demanding and polluting sectors. Since the hospitality industry relies on a steady supply of food for its operations, the supply chain becomes a key factor in managing sustainability. The role-typical questions addressed by the food chain LCA include:

> Is reusable packaging used?
> Does the product carry excessive food miles?
> Are sustainable methods of agriculture used to cultivate the food product?
> Is fresh food being used?

Few hotel companies have yet undertaken a full life-cycle assessment of all their products and services. This is in part due to the cost and complexity of completing a full-scale life-cycle assessment, especially in an industry such as hospitality where numerous products, processes and services form part of the so-called hospitality product. In general, service industries such as the hospitality industry tend to generate less environmental impact throughout their supply and production chain than heavy industries. However, when analyzing the true carbon footprint of hospitality guests, one should consider environmental impacts caused by transport to and from the point of the hospitality product sale.

Despite the service economy accounting for a significant share of the Gross Domestic Product (GDP) of most industrialized countries, LCA models and case studies for service oriented economies have only recently been appearing. Indeed, services present unique challenges for LCA. While LCAs in the hospitality industry are still uncommon, a few case studies have been carried out. The LCAs of hospitality service by Italian hotels (University 'G. G. d'Annunzio Annunzio' and FEBE and FEBE EcoLogic EcoLogic) was performed using the GaBi software (http://www.gabi-software.com/) tool to model life-cycle systems and to process the data. The analysis of data lists the following major impacts:

- Energy use in hotel operations.
- Transport to and from the destination.
- Usage of cleaning materials.
- Other processes such as laundry and waste disposal.

Such case study have pointed towards the potential of various LCA approaches to introduce life-cycle thinking into the decision-making process.

MARKETING RESEARCH

Marketing decision making depends upon the systematic gathering, analysis and interpretation of data for customers and competitors, markets and industries and the broader environment. Numerous agencies have specialized in researching the ethical, social and environmental concerns of consumers. An example of a project focusing on research into consumer behavior and attitudes toward sustainable production and consumption is Sustainable Motivation undertaken by MPG International on behalf of the United Nations Environment Programme (UNEP). Ultimately, the more quality information a business possesses, the better it can adapt and formulate its offer.

PRINCIPLES OF RESPONSIBLE MARKETING

Responsible marketing represents a shift in emphasis away from the traditional approach toward a more ethical understanding that takes a holistic view of the product from cradle to grave and considers the context in which it is produced. It is also concerned about the provision of product information and advice on how to best handle the product and service until disposal.

Every day, the concept of 'the average consumer' loses relevance. In a world of personalized offers and product development, marketing plays an important role. Responsible marketing replies to the increased expectations of consumers wishing to attain a more sustainable level of consumption. Targeting this new generation of consumers is becoming one of the key success factors in the marketing of a product. The marketing mix has now evolved to incorporate the environmental concerns expressed in company policy documents.

Methods of distribution can be adjusted to benefits from the addition of special eco-labeling. Product pricing needs to reflect the possible price variation that results from sustainable production systems. Product promotion can take advantage of the ecological and ethical dimensions. However, a company should not lose sight of the fact that other values such as quality, durability or after-sale service must equally be defended.

Sustainable development should not become the single commercial argument. For the development of a responsible marketing strategy, there are a number of priorities that need to be addressed in the following policy making:

Corporate

Responsible marketing is as much about marketing the organization as any of its products and services. Commitment towards sustainability does not begin with the conception of the product or service level but rather starts at corporate level.

Product/service

Products and services offered within a hotel or restaurant should minimize the use of non-renewable resources and be designed for recyclability. If the manufacturing, or the provision of products and services, is deemed not sustainable, the credibility of the product, the communication and the company are at stake. The best way to sell a product is to be honest about the offer, the sourcing, the production methods and the ingredients.

Packaging

The hospitality industry uses less packaging than other industries. However, hotels and restaurants source food, furniture and fixture, which in turn rely on the massive use of packaging material. A careful analysis of the packaging from the supplier should be made. Preference should be given to products that use less packaging material or to suppliers that have a recycling and re-usage policy. Consideration should be given before using excessive quantities of brochures and guides in promotional activities.

Promotion

Hospitality operations wishing to improve their environmental and social credentials are often eager to communicate their initiatives with customers and other stakeholders to improve the perception of their offer and the company. A note of caution should be made concerning the communication of environmental action and inaction. Environmental inactivity sends out as strong a message as highly profiled environmental activity. Promotion should highlight both company and product credentials in addition to educating the consumer.

Pricing

The additional costs incurred by sustainable production techniques can be passed on to the consumers when environmental and societal gains are communicated. However, when operational costs are reduced following environmental initiatives, such as the traditional hotel towel scheme, it is then ethical to provide a reduction in the final consumer prices.

Transportation and distribution

The issues of product transportation and distribution differ in the hospitality industry even though these activities are essential to daily operations. The act of traveling to and from a destination represents a considerable carbon footprint. Some hotels have taken the initiative to offer guests daily public transport passes that are included in the room rate. Some restaurants source food locally, and cooperate with regional suppliers, in order to reduce food mileage in the sourcing channel.

Quality

Sustainable management requires a shift from quantity towards quality. Quality is part of the environmental profile of a product since goods that last longer consume less natural resources.

Personnel

Awareness of the importance of sustainability in business practices should be enhanced by training and education. Ultimately, the entire workforce is responsible for improvements in sustainable development.

Environmental information

Monitoring improvements to the business brought about by environmental management systems is essential in identifying successes and important challenges. It ensures that suppliers are aligned with corporate requirements and are consistent with environmental policies.

Commercial communication

Company actions are communicated in addition to focusing solely on product or service claims. Publicity should inform, raise awareness and educate customers. Hence, the product and service, the brand and the company build a unique image of a company engaged in sustainable development.

Communication should be divided into several stages:

- Informing consumers
- Listening to consumers
- Giving responsibility to consumers
- reporting and accounting on activities and impacts.

PUBLICITY

Publicity remains one of the most utilized forms of communication of which several kinds can be distinguished.

Daily Publicity

Several forms of daily publicity can be cited. For example, announcing the company vehicles run on gas or electricity. Cities and regions encouraging the use of public transport. Hotels that publicize the use of low energy consumption lighting in guest rooms and public areas.

Traditional Publicity

Traditional publicity seeks to create new trends, values and lifestyles catering to the requests made by consumers who care about the environment. The goal being to associate a feeling of emotion with the given information. Responsible companies are those seeking to limit visual pollution by avoiding the use publicity panels on trucks, taxis or in public transport and sound pollution (while decreasing the amount and time of any visual or radio spots).

Passive Publicity

Passive publicity is achieved by companies that contribute toward humanitarian actions or environmental activities. This type of publicity is most effective for a company seeking to gain recognition for achievements in sustainable development.

Thus, publicity within the context of responsible marketing can take numerous forms: it can transmit a message within the scope of an environmental action and it can also publicize sustainable development activities. Publicity must be designed in a sustainable manner, with respect toward all forms of pollution and environmental damages.

INTERNAL AND EXTERNAL COMMUNICATION

When businesses communicate product information other publics than final consumers are reached. One such internal public are company employees and shareholders. Externally, another group is formed by the political institutions, associations, suppliers and distributors.

INTERNAL COMMUNICATION

The image of a company is not solely based on external communication. Life within a company and the involvement of employees also shape the image projected. Success in a market is the direct result of the work and achievements of its employees. The same is applicable to sustainable development. Environmental initiatives are as successful as the level of employee involvement. There are several internal communication tools available for communicating environmental protection initiatives within the company: Company newsletters, annual sustainability report, notice boards, videos and seminars. The goal being to disseminate information on company programs that seek involvement of all employees.

EXTERNAL COMMUNICATION

A company involved in sustainable development enters into new cooperations with distributors and suppliers and ensures positive relations with environmental organizations and public authorities.

A responsible company creates meaningful relationships with suppliers and distributors whereby the latter commit their businesses to limiting the use of non-renewable resources as well as ensuring ethical work conditions.

A responsible company may find it beneficial to communicate on environmental engagements to public authorities.

Finally, a responsible company will communicate with non-governmental organizations or other consumer protection associations in order to maximize transparency of business activities. Those organizations and associations tend to maintain a close relationship with the media, which can either be very positive or quickly destroy the image of a company if the latter does not keep to its commitments in terms of sustainable development. While maintaining a partnership with an environmental protection association, a company can acquire credibility and legitimacy.

COMPETITIVE ADVANTAGES FROM RESPONSIBLE MARKETING

Responsible marketing strategy helps to:

- Differentiate the brand
- Mitigate risks and identify opportunities
- Increase customer retention and brand loyalty
- Drive innovation and creativity

- Protect reputations and build stronger brands
- Motivate employees
- Retain the best staff
- Delight customers
- Save costs
- Attract investment

GREENWASH – A COMPETITIVE DISADVANTAGE

Another issue managers of hospitality operations have to face is the threat of being accused of *greenwashing*. The term *greenwash 'describes efforts by corporations to portray themselves as environmentally responsible in order to mask environmental wrong doings'* (Whellams and Mac Donald, 2007). Greenwashing can have fatal effects on a company's trustworthiness. Not only a firm's customers are deceived, but greenwash can also ruin relationships with all stakeholders. While competitive advantage can be obtained from sustainable practices and responsible marketing, companies operating in a sustainable way that do not communicate to their external environment face the risk of being overtaken by competitors. A simple example can illustrate this particular situation. Energy Management Systems are implemented in many hotels. The name Energy Management System implies improved energy management and consequently lower energy consumption. This belief is misleading, as Energy Management Systems do not necessarily reduce the energy consumed but more importantly track energy consumption in an accurate way.

If a hotel tries to claim undue credit for environmental protection through its Energy Management system, it could be accused of greenwashing. Companies that greenwash fail to gain competitive advantage and conversely experience competitive disadvantage when the falseness of their actions become known to the public.

Marketing communication about environmental friendliness has to be consistent. Inappropriate responsible marketing techniques have been identified as the 'five routes to failure'. These five doubtful practices and their shortcomings are elaborated in the following table (see Table 8.1).

SUSTAINABLE CLAIMS AND COMMUNICATIONS

Communication is a key element in any marketing process. Accurate information should be communicated to all stakeholders and particularly to customers. The central message should always be clearly understandable,

Table 8.1	Five Routes to Failure of Responsible Marketing	
Dimension	**Description**	**Points of Failure**
Green Spinning	Compartmentalization of sustainable marketing within the PR function, focusing on reputation management	Little effect on product, production or policy decision, thus little real value for the environment and society
Green Selling	*Post hoc* identification of sustainable features in existing products and not seeking new alternatives	Meaningless and unproven green claims put on unchanged products resulting in consumer cynicism and suspicion
Green Harvesting	Use of sustainable technology to save costs (e.g. energy-efficient equipment) to increase profit margins	Cost savings do not filter through to customers and the product is perceived as overly expensive
Enviropreneur Marketing	Existing product range is supplemented with additional 'green lines' without prior in-depth market research of consumer desires	Increasing production orientation and thus hampering long-term market penetration and share
Compliance Marketing	Sustainability initiatives that do not go beyond existing regulations, but are used to promote sustainability credentials	Only a reactive approach, since a company is forced into sustainability practice via legislation

Source: Adapted from Peattie and Crane (2005).

relevant and honest. Companies that promote an environmentally friendly image, products and services must be precise in the claims they make.

In short:

Claims must be *Truthful, accurate and able to be substantiated*. Although there are no requirements to have information independently verified, many hospitality companies work with various standard and certification agencies.

Claims must be *Relevant* to the product or service in question and the impact connected with it.

Claims must be *Clear* about which environmental issue or aspect of the product is referred to. A restaurant may claim to be respectful of the environment because only organic food is used in the kitchen. However, the claim may be irrelevant if the organic products are sourced in far-away countries, necessitating air transportation (air miles).

Claims must be *explicit* about the meaning of any symbol or label used, – unless it is required by law, or is part of an independent certification scheme.

RESPONSIBLE MARKETING: A LOYALTY DRIVER

The principal objective of responsible companies is to create loyalty amongst their customers and develop a sense of concern about issues related to the environment, social equity and responsible consumer behavior. Thus, a company committed to sustainable development should develop a partnership of equality. Logically, the relationship is not simply one of buyer and seller dealing with monetary transaction but rather one of striving for the common and greater good.

CHAPTER QUESTIONS

1. Identify the principles of responsible marketing for hotels and restaurants.
2. Explain Life-Cycle Assessment and its possible applications in the hospitality industry.
3. Identify the competitive advantage of hospitality companies embracing responsible marketing strategies.

READING LIST

Dinan, C., Sargeant, A., 2000. Social marketing and sustainable tourism – is there a match? Int J Tourism Res 2, 1–14.

Fuller, D.A., 1999. Sustainable marketing: managerial – ecological issues. Sage Publications, Inc, Thousand Oaks, CA.

GaBi Software <http://www.gabisoftware.com/>

Kotler, P., Bowen, J., Makens, J., 2003. Marketing for Hospitality and Tourism, Third ed. Prentice Hall, NJ.

Kotler, P., Roberto, N., Lee, N., 2002. Social marketing: improving the quality of life, 2nd ed. Sage Publications, Inc, Thousand Oaks, CA.

Middleton, V.T.C., Hawkins, R., 1998. Sustainable Tourism: A Marketing Perspective. Butterworth-Heinemann, Oxford.

Peattie, K., Crane, A., 2005. Environmentally Responsible Marketing: Legend, Myth, Farce or Prophesy? Qualitative Market Research: An International Journal 8 (4), 357–370.

Whellams, M., MacDonald, C., 2007. Greenwashing. In Robert Kolb (ed.), Encyclopedia of Business Ethics and Society. Newbury Park, CA: Sage.

Williams, E., 2008. *CSR Europe's Sustainable Marketing Guide*. CSR Europe, Brussels.

CHAPTER 9

Responsible Consumerism

Study Objectives

- To examine the changes in consumer behavior in relation to sustainable development
- To identify the various types of consumers
- To provide an understanding of the importance for companies in tourism and identify the motives of the responsible tourist
- To provide an understanding of the concept of sustainable development in relation to external communications and responsible marketing
- To appreciate the development of a new consumption model

CONTENTS

Consumers are the crux of responsible consumption. Today's consumers influence companies and public authorities in various ways; as simple consumers with their purchasing habits, as investors in companies engaged in environmental protection and as citizens electing governments that support sustainable policies. A significant and growing proportion of consumers support the concept of sustainable development. Consumers are increasingly vigilant in regard to the ethical behavior of businesses. Society is now entering a new business paradigm, emphasis on the unique race towards profits is being modified to incorporate the race towards saving the planet. The general public is increasingly supportive of business strategy that favorizes social welfare and environmental protection.

THE ENGAGED CONSUMER

Consumer behavior and attitudes have changed over the last three decades in regards to the awareness of sustainability of products and services. Consumers, not governments, are the driving force behind the trend of companies to develop environmental stewardship. Firms that neglect consumer attitudes fail to satisfy their needs. Hotel customers can be basically divided into two groups: corporate and leisure guests. Both groups show very distinct booking and spending behavior. Green thinking is altering the way all hotel guests contemplate the hospitality experience. The effect of 'green thinking' forces hoteliers to respond to changed needs and wants.

In the first analysis a consumer is an individual who acquires a product or service for personal usage. Consumption is not a matter of freedom of choices anymore, but is closely related to issues of responsible citizenship. There is an emergence of a new type of consumer: the engaged consumer who invests his individual responsibility in social equity and responsibility for the environment. The engaged consumer seeks control of his values and, in particular, tries to ensure value for money by purchasing from retailers with short supply and distribution systems. There are two types of engaged consumer: the activist consumer and the informed consumer.

The activist

Consumers that display activism oblige companies to engage in sustainable business practices. Activist consumers strongly engage in favor of sustainable development. Sorting waste, safeguarding energy by simple gestures, buying biodegradable products, using public or human-powered transport, consuming organic, local food, composting, participating in ecotourism projects and volunteering for environmental or local social associations are simple examples of what is considered common sense by the activist consumer. The activist will prefer to participate in local food cooperatives that trade with local farmers rather than purchase organic products in supermarkets. Some activists will visit farmers' markets at closing time in order to gather fruit and vegetable leftovers often deemed as not *saleable* because of minor faults. Lastly, the typical activist consumer participates in large gatherings to discuss lifestyle experiences, contemplate new ideas and generally have open exchanges within the community of other activists.

The informed

Despite the rise of the activist consumer, there are signs of a small decline in this trend in society. Intensive media coverage of environmental issues has brought about changes of perception and is influencing patterns of consumption. The trend is now to consume less but better, with a preference for durable, utilitarian products and services. Due to the plethora of multiple news media e.g. the Internet, Blogs, Networks, Twitters, consumers now have the possibility of obtaining quicker and more pertinent product information than ever before. The informed consumer requires a personalized service with special requirements: lisibility and traceability of the labels found on products. He or she observes closely how and where products are manufactured and supports a return to the concept of sustainable food e.g. organic production. The informed consumer tends to be less politically motivated but will focus attention on raising the awareness of social equity and the environment within the community at large.

CONSUMERS AND SUSTAINABLE DEVELOPMENT

As we have seen, the activist and the informed consumer, involve themselves in the safeguard of the environment and more particularly in sustainable development. Serious environmental degradation and extensive media coverage has raised a collective awakening amongst consumers which has in turn altered priorities in the lives of individuals and in consumption habits. Post-war consumerism has been about the purchase of disposable consumer goods and the idea and of purchasing as a form of leisure activity to satisfy spontaneous emotional wants. However, those wants are infinite and as soon as they are appeased, reappear again.

This endless spiral of consumption satisfaction and frustration has pushed consumers to a new paradigm of consumption. Society is witnessing a return to products and service authenticity that is coupled with a desire to purchase locally. Alternative forms of energy sourcing and the purchasing of equitable products are other signs of growing interest in sustainable consumerism.

Unpredictable consumers

A new type of consumers has now appeared who has a clear preference for mass consumption. It is the unpredictable consumer. This incoherent consumer is not an activist, not particularly informed and rather unaware of the impact choices make when purchasing products and services. This consumer is unpredictable in his or her purchasing behavior. Consumption depends on a variety of emotional and non emotional factors. Such consumers may wear a very expensive watch, drive a luxury car but do the weekly food purchases at the mass discounter. Awareness of sustainability is often limited but the retailer is presented with the possibility educate and promote sustainable goods to this type of consumer.

The greening of tourists

Tourist interest in the environment has gradually increased over the past few decades. A study was carried out by the Virginia Polytechnic Institute and State University in which 489 air travelers were asked about their views on environmentally sustainable hotels. Seventy percent claimed they would choose a hotel with a strong environmental record rather than an ordinary hotel, and only 3% had an negative opinion on environmentally sustainable hotels. This illustrates the importance of customer interest in environmentally conscious hotels.

Ecotourists

For many, mass tourism has already gone too far. A new phenomenon has developed over the last decade in the field of tourism: ecotourism. Although ecotourism accounted for a very small percentage of all international travel expenditure, it is fastest growing and a lucrative segment of tourism. Eco-tourists are tagged as high spending, nature-loving, responsible and are undoubtedly an attractive option for governments looking for ways of earning foreign exchange. The word 'ecotourism' sounds pleasing to the ear. Finally, it is a form of tourism that takes into consideration the needs of the environment and not only the needs of the tourist. Ecotourism is tailor-made for individuals wishing to escape overcrowding and the environmental impacts that are associated with mass tourism. It is a new model of destination development, that seeks to harmonize the tourist with local society and the local environment. However, questions arise over the eco-authenticity of four-wheel-drive vehicles racing through Africa's renowned game parks. Is trekking considered as ecotourism when authorities build a road through an boreal forest to reach a trekking lodge? Is ecotourism a marketing ploy for tour operatsors rather than a statement of true commitment? Are struggling nations around the world able to resist compromising their environment and their culture when they lure affluent foreigners and their dollars? Ecotourism is possibly the most overused and misused word in the tourism industry.

Swarbrooke and Horner (2007) define ecotourists as largely moti-vated to see the natural history of a destination typically with the purpose of observing wildlife and learning something about the environment. The term 'shades of green tourists' is represented in Figure 9.1. It is argued that environmental awareness is different amongst individuals when considering the broad range of environmental concern. It is also argued that a tourist's

Not at all green	Light green	Dark green	Totally green
Read what holiday brochures say about green issues and sustainable tourism	Think about green issues and try to reduce normal water consumption in destinations where water is scarce	Consciously seek to find out more about a particular issue and become more actively involved in the issue by joining a pressure group for example	Read what holiday brochures say about green issues and sustainable tourism Use public transport to get to destinations and travel on while on holiday Boycott hotels, which have a poor reputation on environmental issues	Pay to go on holiday to work on a conservation project

Do not take holiday from home at all so as not to harm the environment in any way as a tourist |

No sacrifices made because of views	No sacrifices made because of views	No sacrifices made because of views

Shallow interest in all green issues	Deep interest in all green issues/or one in particular

Large proportion of the population	Small proportion of the population

FIGURE 9.1 *Shades of green tourism. (Reprinted by permission of Butterworth-Heinemann. From "Consumer behaviour in tourism" by Swarbrooke, J. and Horner, S., 2007.) Copyright © 2007 by Butterworth-Heinemann; all rights reserved.*

attitudes regarding environmental issues are highly dependent on where he or she originally comes from (Ivarsson, 1998; Swarbrooke and Horner, 2007). Similarly, a hotel's performance on environmental issues is highly dependent on where its core guests come from. Greek hoteliers, for example, have greatly improved with regard to their environmental performance because the major part of their guests come from Germany where environmental protection and awareness are high. Within Europe, the Scandinavian countries, Germany, France and the Netherlands are far more concerned about environmental issues than eastern or southern member countries. Internationally operating hotel chains accommodate guests from various countries and cultures. This variety creates an issue in a way that different guests have different environmental perceptions and standards. Each guest has his or her own perception of sound environmental management. Additionally, there are different opinions on to what extent guests should be involved in environmentally sustainable initiatives. By promoting research, guidelines to tour operators and code for travelers, the hopes are that eco-tourism can gain the place it deserves in the future of tourism development.

Responsible tourists

The concept of the responsible tourist is based on the relationship that is established between the tourist and the tourism actors, whether it is the providers of tourism experiences, hotel employees or local inhabitants. The tourist not only travels with his own culture, practices, attitudes and financial capacity, but also he or she brings along curiosity and a desire for exchanges. The welcoming communities are more than local accommodation facilities. Rather, it is a village, an area or a region with its population, its own social rules, its own economy and its own environment. The relationship created, a mixture of curiosity and respect between the host and the guest, constitutes the first step of responsible tourism.

More sophisticated than the mass tourism product which may include transport, lodging and activities at the destination, responsible tourism falls under a logic of sustainable development. Indeed, it is located at the intersection of three fields: economic, social and environmental. Responsible tourism, in its design, involves the local population, stimulates local agricultural, supports local artisans and generates incomes that contribute to the financing of new infrastructure (education, health, environment and productions). Responsible tourism is an element of societal dynamics leading to discovery, exchanges and respect. The responsible tourist is a vector of solidarity between individuals of different cultures. Lastly, the responsible tourist is a link in the chain of events that lead to protection of heritage, natural resources and the environment for future generations. The responsible tourist acts as a mini-laboratory of sustainable development.

MOTIVATIONS FOR RESPONSIBLE CONSUMER BEHAVIOR: SOME THEORETICAL CONSIDERATIONS

If an individual regards his potential contribution to humanity and environmental equilibrium as being effective, the relationship between his or her attitudes and his actions go in parallel. If on the contrary, the individual does not recognize these impacts, attitudes and behavior will diverge. When an individual perceives his or her effectiveness at controlling the overall impacts on the environment, his or her sense of responsibility increases. Conversely when an individual's ability to control the impact of the environment is disenfranchised, the behavior of that individual becomes irrational.

Attitudes, intentions and actual consumption behavior

These theoretical considerations make it possible to explain the shift between attitudes, intentions and the actual behavior of consumers. The more the consumer estimates that he is responsible for societal or environmental problems, the more he has the feeling that his actions – even in minute dosage – have a direct benefit, which is recognized by peers. However, the more the consumer believes in responsibility to society, the more his behavior will reflect his attitudes. Human beings constantly try to attain coherence in their behavior. When an individual accepts that external factors influence his or her behavior, the more his or her consumption habits will be disproportionate to his or her attitudes.

An individual with a compelling sense of self-responsibility will search for products which mirror his or her attitudes. Consequently, if environmental protection and support of local economies are high on an individual's agenda, products that have corresponding characteristics will be favored and purchased. The study of consumer behavior provides businesses with a detailed framework of analysis. A clear understanding of such a framework is essential for companies wanting to increase their performance on the three sustainability pillars.

The tourist's intentional and actual consumption behavior

The travel and tourism industry is the largest industry and is still growing. Competition is fierce. Businesses that assume they are riding an automatic growth escalator invariably descend into stagnation (Levitt, 1960). Consumers have a growing influence on the development of sustainable investments made in the hotel industry. Contradicting results have been published about consumer buying behavior regarding sustainability in the industry. For example, Miller's (2003) research showed that 'consumers are already making decisions based on environmental, social and economic quality for day-to-day products and are keen to transfer these habits to the purchase of tourism products' (Miller, 2003: 17). Miller's research shows that 78% of respondents did either always or sometimes look for environmental information about their intended holiday destination (Miller, 2003: 29). The Italian Environment Protection Agency reported that interest in eco-labels has increased and that 73% of interviewees preferred eco-labeled tourist accommodation (ANPA, 2001). Conversely, Reiser *et al.* reported that 'tourists' decision making is still only marginally influenced by such [eco] labels and it appears that sustainability does not feature much in tourists' general consumption behaviour' (Reiser *et al.*, 2005: 590). Tourists' willingness to pay, or purchase intentions do not always reflect their actual buying behavior.

The cost-saving dilemma

Promoting environmentally sustainability actions to hotel guests can be a delicate topic.

Initiatives such as towel reuse schemes and energy efficient technology result in vast cost reductions.

The savings in operational costs may not be reflected in lower room rates. Consequently, if hospitality operations promote cost savings from environmentally sustainable initiatives, guests may criticize the hotels' pricing policy. Some hospitality managers believe that such environmental actions result in negative customer reaction (Stipanuk, 2002). This proves to be particularly true if sustainability initiatives reduce the guest level of comfort. In such circumstances, hotel guests look for new service providers.

A new market segment

LOHAS is an acronym for Lifestyles of Health and Sustainability – a multi-billion market segment in the United States alone. LOHAS aligns itself with groups such as New Age belief (based on Eastern religions e.g. Buddhism, Pantheism or Hinduism, and on the harmony between individuals and nature) with environmentalist interest groups and the alternative medicine movement. It is a marketplace for goods and services that appeal to consumers who value health, the environment, social justice, personal development and sustainable living.

These consumers are variously referred to as culturally creative, conscious citizens who are willing to pay more for goods that are deemed sustainable. Approximately 19% of the adults in the United States alone are currently considered LOHAS (LOHAS, 2009). These consumers represent a target segment for the organic food industry and destinations focused on cultural offers.

LOHAS' rival is the LOVOS. LOVOS stands for 'Lifestyle of Voluntary Simplicity.' This segment is oriented toward health and sustainability.

Highly critical of consumerism, the LOVOS associate environmental awareness with environmentally suitable behavior. From a marketing point of view, the LOVOS is a marginal phenomenon that is neglected.

The influences of labels and certification schemes on the consumer's buying or purchasing behavior

Similar to all industry sectors, the hospitality industry strives to create a positive image conveying values matching those of the targeted consumers. This image has four dimensions: *financial, commercial, social and societal*.

- The *financial dimension* concerns the owners and shareholders. It is concerned with transparency, clarity and reliability of the information.

- The *commercial dimension* is concerned with consumers' wallets. It encourages fair trade, fair value of products and services rendered.

- The *social dimension* is concerned with the motivation of the employees. It relates to the conditions of employment, the remuneration aspect and the working climate.

- The *societal dimension* is concerned with all other partners (suppliers, distributors, associations, public authorities). It confers a professional and responsible image and encourages cooperation.

Image contributes directly to business sustainability and in turn commercial viability. A business that makes the decision to invest in environmental and social responsibility can gain precious points in terms of image. Equally, a proper and recognized certification or eco-label enhances a company's marketing presence.

However, opinions are divided on whether or not a certified product or service automatically represents better quality than its traditional, non-certified counterpart. Consumers may perceive certified product as being too expensive. Consumers tend to pay greater attention to labeling and certification schemes for basic items such as food rather than for other luxury products. Intense media coverage on food and health issues is the key driver for raising awareness in society at large. Consequently, consumers may pay more attention to the organic labeling of food bought at the local store compared to the ISO14001 accreditation obtained by the hotelier around the corner. Consumers find it also difficult to personally check whether the standards prescribed within the certification scheme are actually respected. Trust is a key element in the acceptance and purchasing of certified or labeled products and services.

A strategy of correct information and transparency needs to be put in place in the whole area of environmental certification in order to obtain the desired impact on consumers.

RESPONSIBLE CONSUMER BEHAVIOR: CONSUMPTION MODEL

Personal purchase choices can be structured around individual determinants including physiological state, preferences, knowledge, perceptions and other psychological factors. Individual determinants alone are not sufficient to explain responsible purchasing behavior. Public policies, social interactions, economic situation and the physical environment build the collective determinants of responsible purchasing behavior. Numerous frameworks have been developed for analyzing consumption. All these frameworks are based on the simple fact that consumers making choices are influenced by numerous factors. These can be categorized in person-related factors (sociodemographics, biological, psychological), environmental factors (cultural, economic, marketing) and factors concerning the intrinsic the properties of the product or service (physiological effects, sensory perception). Responsible consumerism is a holistic approach to understanding influences on consumption. Motivations for responsible consumerism can be summarized in four dimensions, as described in Figure 9.2, namely **personal health**, **ecology**, **ethics** and **lifestyle**.

The decision process can be described as a fairly linear progression starting with the recognition of a need, followed by a search for information, the evaluation stage and the choice (Traill, 1999). A series of influencing factors plays a critical role before, during and after the purchasing decision process as portrayed in Figure 9.2, thus, forming the *eight Ps* that influence the responsible customer's choice. **Personal experience** can be seen as the sensory attributes of a product, such as the tasting experience in a restaurant or individual food preferences. **Publicity** influences consumers by the methods used to market and promote hotels and restaurants. The **press** through media coverage of hotel and restaurant rating and ranking schemes and by news on the latest popular or exotic destination, is also an influencing element. **Production methods** from the transformation processes of food in the hotel kitchen to the type of equipment used and the energy consumed play a role in the final choice of the responsible consumer. The **product chain** has become an important aspect of sustainable business practices. The use of fertilizers and pesticides in growing foodstuff, as well

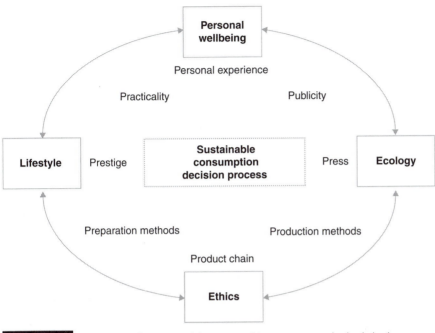

FIGURE 9.2 *Persuasive influences model on responsible consumer purchasing behavior.*

as processing, packaging and distribution have become critical influencing factors in the responsible decision process.

The remaining *three Ps* of the persuasive influences model in Figure 9.2, namely the **preparation methods** (cooking and waste management), **prestige** (following social trends and norms) and **practicality** (purchasing convenience, cost and other constraints) also have an equally important effect.

The inherent dynamic structure of the model allows for the decision process to be modeled according to the various life stages and the strength of one influencing factor over another over time.

Kids – born as responsible consumers

Physiological changes take place as childhood passes to the early years of adult life. As a result of emotional and social development, young people exert more control over purchasing choices. It is especially younger individuals that are likely to respond to environmental issues. Today's children grow up in times where environmental, economic and social issues are converging. Hopefully, future generations will adopt responsible consumerism as the only possible type of consumption.

CHAPTER QUESTIONS

1. In which way does understanding the motivations of the responsible tourist influence products and services on offer?

2. How can a hotel or restaurant cater to the responsible tourist?

3. Identify the eight Ps of the responsible customer's choice and explain how they work using an example from the hospitality industry.

READING LIST

Bohdanowicz, P., 2005. European hoteliers' environmental attitudes: greening the business. Cornell Hotel and Restaurant Administration Quarterly 46 (2), 188–204.

Dolnicar, S., Crouch, G.I., Long, P., 2008. Environment-friendly tourists: what do we really know about them? J. Sustain. Tourism 16 (2), 197–210.

France, L., 1997. Earthscan reader in sustainable tourism. Earthscan, London.

Grove, S.J., Fisk, R.P., Pickett, G.M., Kangun, N., 1996. Going Green in the service sector. Eur. J. Market. 30 (5), 56–66.

Honey, M., 1999. Ecotourism and Sustainable Development: Who Owns Paradise? first ed. Island Press, Washington, DC.

Honey, M., 2008. Ecotourism and Sustainable Development: Who Owns Paradise? second ed. Island Press, Washington, DC.

Levitt, T., 1960. Marketing myopia. Harvard Business Review 38, 45–56.

LOHAS, 2009. LOHAS Background. Louisville, CO: Lifestyle of health and sustainability. Available at: http://www.lohas.com/.

McDonald, S., Oates, C.J., Young, C., Hwang, K., 2006. Towards sustainable consumption: researching voluntary simplifiers. Psychol. Market. 23 (6), 515–534.

McLaren, D., 2003. Rethinking Tourism and Ecotravel, second ed. Kumarian Press, Sterling, VA.

Miller, G., 2003. Consumerism in sustainable tourism: a survey of UK consumers. J. Sustain. Tourism 11 (1), 17–39.

Reiser, A., Simmons, D.G., 2005. A quasi-experimental method for testing the effectiveness of ecolabel promotion. J. Sustain. Tourism 13 (6), 590–616.

Richards, G. (Ed.), 2001. Cultural Attractions and European Tourism. CABI Publishing, Wallingford, UK.

Stipanuk, D.M., 2002. Hospitality Facilities Management and Design. Educational Institute of the American Hotel and Lodging Association, Lansing.

Swabrooke, J., Horner, S., 2007. Consumer Behaviour in Tourism, second ed. Elsevier, Oxford.

TIES, 2002. Definitions and principles. The International Ecotourism Society, Washingon, DC Available at: http://www.ecotourism.org/webmodules/webarticlesnet/templates/eco_template.aspx?articleid = 95&zoneid = 2.

Traill, B.W., 1999. Prospect for the future: nutritional, environmental and sustainable food production considerations-changes in cultural and consumer habits. In Proc Conference on International Food Trade, Melbourne, 11–15 October.

Weaver, D., 2005. Sustainable Tourism. Butterworth-Heinemann, Oxford.

CHAPTER 10

Corporate Social Responsibility for Sustainable Business Management

Study Objectives

- To identify the underlying principles of sustainable business management
- To define corporate social responsibility
- To identify the relevance of corporate social responsibility to the hotel and restaurant industry

BUSINESS CHARTER FOR SUSTAINABLE DEVELOPMENT

For many hospitality managers, the daily agenda still focuses on priorities seen to be more important than sustainable business management, including cost control, profit maximization and shareholder value. But in the context of globalization, emerging sustainable development concerns and priorities increasingly cut across all areas of management interest and responsibility. Environmental protection, social accountability, ethics and education, sustainable development and think global, act local proposals are examples of intertwined matters redrawing the rules: doing business in the twenty-first century is different. Owners, general managers and line managers cannot ignore these developments. They need to understand and respond to changing societal expectations of business. And they must effectively communicate what they consider to be realistic expectations of what business can – and cannot – achieve. In this chapter, we will be looking at one particular aspect of doing business in the new century. Corporate Social Responsibility (CSR) is concerned with a company's obligations to be accountable to all its stakeholders when operating and undertaking business activities.

The world business environment is on the move. The last 50 years have been a real whirlwind in terms of management change. What defined business requirements for success and competitiveness yesterday may be quite different today. Indeed, various trends and forces are challenging the conventional views of competitiveness and of the success factors for prosperity. This is particularly true for hospitality and food-and-beverage operations, which depend on a complex supply chain and on an intricate delivery network. Generally speaking, the following trends and forces affect businesses:

- Globalization of markets
- Globalization of supply chains and financial flows
- Intensification of competition
- Quantum leaps in technological development
- Advances in information technology
- Demographic changes
- Environmental challenges
- Changing lifestyles and value systems

There is a widespread recognition in the hospitality industry that environmental protection must be among the highest priorities. The hospitality industry generally favors a self-regulation system, while governments often prefer to legislate. The International Chamber of Commerce (ICC) created a Business Charter for Sustainable Development comprising 16 principles for environmental management (see Table 10.1), one of the fundamental aspects of sustainable management.

A company deciding to endorse the charter will utilise the principles to improve environmental management within the organisation and to help determine which principles should be included the company's own Environmental Management System (EMS). The principles then act as a guidance tool. Detailed standards should be listed and explained in the EMS and companies are usually measured against an industry standard or code. Consequently, the challenge of hospitality managers is to regularly demonstrate and document their actions and achievements. Hospitality operations seeking to engage actively with their staff and communities, referring to principle 14 in Table 10.1, need to define the parameters in order to report the outcome of the activities undertaken in both financial and social terms. The ICC developed the charter in 1991 when environmental management by businesses was only starting to rise in importance. By today's standard it is necessary to add the social dimension of sustainable development.

Table 10.1	Business Charter for Sustainable Development by the International Chamber of Commerce
Principles	**Explanation**
1. Corporate priority	To recognize environmental management as among the highest corporate priorities and as a key determinant to sustainable development; to establish policies, programs and practices for conducting operations in an environmentally sound manner.
2. Integrated management	To integrate these policies, programs and practices fully into each business as an essential element of management in all its functions.
3. Process of improvement	To continue to improve corporate policies, programs and environmental performance, taking into account technical developments, scientific understanding, consumer needs and community expectations, with legal regulations as a starting point; and to apply the same environmental criteria internationally.
4. Employee education	To educate, train and motivate employees to conduct their activities in an environmentally responsible manner.
5. Prior assessment	To assess environmental impacts before starting a new activity or project and before decommissioning a facility or leaving a site.
6. Products and services	To develop and provide products or services that have no undue environmental impact and are safe in their intended use, that are efficient in their consumption of energy and natural resources and that can be recycled, reused or disposed of safely.
7. Customer advice	To advise, and where relevant educate, customers, distributors and the public in the safe use, transportation, storage and disposal of products provided; and to apply similar considerations to the provision of services.
8. Facilities and operations	To develop, design and operate facilities and conduct activities taking into consideration the efficient use of energy and materials, the sustainable use of renewable resources, the minimization of adverse environmental impact and waste generation and the safe and responsible disposal of residual wastes.
9. Research	To conduct or support research on the environmental impacts of raw materials, products, processes, emissions and wastes associated with the enterprise and on the means of minimizing such adverse impacts.
10. Precautionary approach	To modify the manufacture, marketing or use of products or services or the conduct of activities, consistent with scientific and technical understanding, to prevent serious or irreversible environmental degradation.
11. Contractors and suppliers	To promote the adoption of these principles by contractors acting on behalf of the enterprise, encouraging and, where appropriate, requiring improvements in their practices to make them consistent with those of the enterprise; and to encourage the wider adoption of these principles by suppliers.
12. Emergency preparedness	To develop and maintain, where significant hazards exist, emergency preparedness plans in conjunction with the emergency services, relevant authorities and the local community, recognizing potential trans-boundary impacts.
13. Transfer of technology	To contribute to the transfer of environmentally sound technology and management methods throughout the industrial and public sectors.
14. Contributing to the common effort	To contribute to the development of public policy and to business, governmental and intergovernmental programs and educational initiatives that will enhance environmental awareness and protection.
15. Openness to concerns	To foster openness and dialog with employees and the public, anticipating and responding to their concerns about the potential hazards and impacts of operations, products, wastes or services, including those of trans-boundary or global significance.
16. Compliance and reporting	To measure environmental performance; to conduct regular environmental audits and assessments of compliance with company requirements, legal requirements and these principles; and to periodically provide appropriate information to the Board of Directors, shareholders, employees, the authorities and the public.

Source: http://www.iccwbo.org/policy/environment/.

CORPORATE SOCIAL RESPONSIBILITY (CSR): DEFINITION AND DIMENSION

Corporate Social Responsibility (CSR) – also referred to as business ethics, corporate citizenship and corporate accountability – is a concept by which companies integrate the interests and needs of customers, employees, suppliers, shareholders, communities and the planet into corporate strategies (Palazzi and Starcher, 2001). In short, businesses need to be good corporate citizens. This implies that corporations need to rethink the reason they exist in a way that lightens their impact (Brown, 2001) on the local surroundings while operating in a progressively more global setting. In the past, the social dimension of sustainability has often been neglected and most often businesses focused on implementing environmentally sustainable strategies (Omann and Spangenberg, 2002). But 'to be a good corporate citizen implies more than just responsible environmental operation: it requires positive engagement in the community in a number of ways'

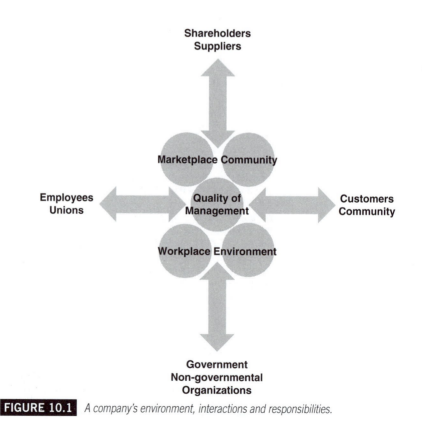

FIGURE 10.1 *A company's environment, interactions and responsibilities.*

(Green Hotelier, 2000: 10). A sustainable business has to ensure to positively contribute to the development of all others it affects.

We can then sum up the environment in which companies take responsibilities under the CSR concept, as depicted in Figure 10.1.

These responsibilities form the CSR dimensions, and CSR is all about managing these responsibilities.

SHAREHOLDERS' VALUE AND INTERESTS

Maximization of shareholders' value is at the core of corporation strategy, but not exclusively. It is often at the moment of collision between the interests of the shareholders and that of the community that corporations come under extreme pressure. Indeed, no companies can still allow themselves to choose the narrow interests of the shareholders over the broader interests of the community. Kenneth Boulding's essay in 1966 titled *The Economics of the Coming Spaceship Earth* boldly suggested that problems result from acting like cowboys on a limitless open frontier, the cowboy economy, when in truth we inhabit a living spaceship with a finely balanced life-support system. Via communication technology, communities are linked together. Thus, a growing number of consumers are aware of the *cowboy* attitude of some businesses and are demanding more information about how products are made, how food-and-beverage operations are run or how employees are being treated. A number of companies have been caught doing what was considered wrong by civil society and have paid a high price in terms of reputation and future sales. In short, these companies have failed to meet the demand for social responsibility.

Suppliers

A firm is vulnerable to the weakest link in its supply chain. Like-minded companies can form profitable long-term business relationships by improving standards, and thereby reducing risks. Larger hospitality firms can stimulate smaller firms with whom they do business to implement a CSR approach. For example, some large hospitality companies require their food suppliers to comply with worker codes and standards.

Customers

Changing unsustainable patterns of consumption is widely seen as an important driver to achieving sustainable development. Companies play an essential role by developing an honest and transparent relationship with consumers. There is a need for consumers to understand the links between a healthy local economy, an attractive and balanced environment and food products. Indeed, consumers are increasingly interested in the sourcing of the foodstuff but also in the transformation processes within the food and beverage supply chain. Guest education as well as labeling on the menu is important, inspiring the customers for healthier nutrition. A hands-on example can be the herb-and-vegetable garden of a restaurant which could be used for educating guests about the quality of local and seasonal produce. There are multiple examples of initiatives to bring local farmers and customers together, and hence benefit the local economy. These include 'local market' events, where local farmers offer their 'food from the land' in the restaurant establishment. Hospitality operation web sites should also be used for providing information on initiatives in sustainability thereby educating guests in regard to products, services, suppliers etc.

An effective way to educate the customer is to bring out the message of sustainability in the overall atmosphere of the hospitality operation. While the decoration, furniture and landscaping around the buildings can be used to enhance the idea of sustainability, offering extended tours of the 'back-of-the-house' operations will contribute to the guests' general understanding of the critical issues.

Additionally, it should be possible for guests to take part, on a voluntary basis, in some community development projects and environmental programs. Options to raise money for social community development projects could be through a donation box with information on the supported project.

Community

Ways to make the local community benefit from the presence of an establishment should be identified. Support through development projects with time, money or other needed resources could be options. Waste furniture and fittings resulting from refurbishments could be reused by local charities and other businesses and food leftovers could be given to homeless people or charities. Being sensitive to the needs of the local community also includes respecting their cultural heritage as well as traditions. Purchasing local artists' or craftspeople's items and displaying them for sale in the hotel lobby or the restaurant is also supportive. Garden pots and ornaments also could be selected from local producers, used for decoration or offered for sale as 'locally made' products (Green Hotelier, 2006a). Initiatives like these would allow the restaurants' customers interact with parts of the wider community, a very important aspect in regard to social sustainability (Wilkinson, 1991).

Government

The roles for a business in the modern global economy are diverse from maximizing profits and shareholder value, to being accountable to stakeholders and to contributing to a better world. What were once guiding principles of governments have become the responsibility of enterprises too and where internal issues surrounding the adoption of CSR are fundamental, CSR is subject to laws, regulations, norms and customs of a country. Because humans do not live in one restricted area, nor are countries under one type of supra-national governance, at least not in practice, CSR faces the global challenge of adapting to constantly changing situations. From environmental protection to child labor, employment practices and labor standards, national governments often set what is considered the base by which every organization within the national borders must abide to. Are there any obligations beyond the law? This is a very important question raised over the last decade.

Roger L. Martin from the Rotman School of Management proposes a Corporate Virtue Matrix, as represented in Figure 10.2. The matrix can guide us in understanding of what constitutes CSR behavior in one region in comparison to another. The matrix depicts the forces that generate CSR. Martin explains that the *civil foundation*, the bottom two quadrants in the matrix, represent the norms, customs and regulations that govern corporate practices. Companies may decide to engage in these practices by *choice* in choosing to conform to the norms and customs or in *compliance* by being forced to abide by the law or regulations. Basically, the *instrumental* behavior of a company in the civil foundation 'does no more than meet society's baseline expectations' (Martin, 2002), serving the cause of shareholder value.

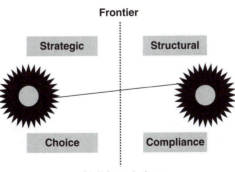

FIGURE 10.2 *The Virtue Matrix (Reprinted by permission of Harvard Business Review. From "The virtue matrix: calculating the return on corporate responsibility" by Martin, R.L., 80(3) 2002.) Copyright © 2002 by the Harvard Business School Publishing Corporation; all rights reserved.*

The matrix's upper quadrants illustrate the *frontier*, whereby companies demonstrate innovation in terms of socially responsible behavior. Corporate behavior is described as being intrinsic. Maximization of shareholders' value combined with supply of social responsibility behavior is a *strategic frontier*. Other activities benefiting society at large except for shareholders are located in the *structural frontier*. Behaviors from the *frontier* can migrate to the *civil foundation* as time goes by. Health and dental benefits were once part of the frontier quadrants for German workers, as very few companies offered these social advantages. Such behavior from a few corporations was soon to be imitated by many and finally, these benefits moved into the *civil foundation*. The border between *frontier* and *civil foundation* moves upward when new CSR behavior actions are adopted and widely imitated or when governing bodies legislate in favor of higher CSR standards or control.

The Corporate Virtue Matrix can be useful when looking at CSR on a global scale. It allows for understanding which corporate behavior can average up the *civil foundation* in countries suffering from troubled economic and social development. On the other hand, the matrix does not prevent the *civil foundation* border of a country from going down, with tragic consequences.

Non-governmental organizations (NGOs)

Non-governmental organization is a term that has become widely accepted for referring to a non-profit making, voluntary, service-oriented or development-oriented organization, either for the benefit of members (a grassroots organization) or of other members of the population (e.g. agency). A non-profit group or association is organized outside of institutionalized political structures to realize particular social objectives (such as environmental protection) or serve particular constituencies (such as indigenous people). NGO activities range from research, information distribution, training, local organization and community service to legal advocacy, lobbying for legislative change and civil disobedience. In the cases in which NGOs are funded totally or partially by governments, the NGO maintains its non-governmental status insofar as it excludes government representatives from membership in the organization.

NGOs have played a crucial role in sustainable development. This is partly the result of restructuring waves of the welfare system in many Western countries and the drive toward globalization. In a nutshell, many problems cannot be solved within a nation. International treaties and international organizations such as the World Trade Organization were perceived as being too centered on the interests of capitalist enterprises. Some argued that in an attempt to counterbalance this trend, NGOs have developed to emphasize humanitarian issues, developmental aid and sustainable development. A prominent example of this is the World Social Forum, which is a rival convention to the World Economic Forum held annually in January in Davos, Switzerland.

NGOs today play often a consultative and lobbying role in pushing for stricter governmental legislation and business obligations on all sustainability issues.

Employees

In order to make the local community benefit most, employees should be local wherever possible. If necessary, local workers should be trained in order to place them into respective positions. Being sensitive to the needs of the employees and treating them in a fair manner is also of great importance. This includes ensuring a safe working environment, paying fair wages etc (Green Hotelier, 2007a).

The best environmental policy does not help much if employees do not understand the philosophy and the goals behind it and do not know how to attain the goals. Employees, expected to achieve and implement certain initiatives, need to have proper skills, knowledge, motivation and awareness thereof (Green Hotelier, 2007b). Hence, environmental training should be regularly conducted, be enjoyable as well as involve and motivate staff in order to achieve best results. Once environmental data on special projects is available, targets for staff should be set in special training sessions and feedback should be given thereon. Environmental training could include topics such as waste management, introducing the importance of reducing, reusing and recycling to the staff and pushing them to give some good suggestions. To improve training results even more, a copy of the operations sustainability policy could be given to each employee and information could be displayed on staff notice boards. A small library with books, journals and additional information on recent environmental topics could be established for all employees (Green Hotelier, 2006c, 2007a). Allocating money saved through environmental initiatives to a special staff fund could be an option to motivate staff even more to implement certain practices. In order to encourage creative ideas from employees, suggestion boxes, competitions or special rewards could be used (Green Hotelier, 2007a).

Unions

Regarding the internal aspects of CSR, the right of freedom of association, collective bargaining and complaints procedures are granted. A labor union is an organization run by and for employees who have joined together to achieve common goals in key areas such as wages, hours and working conditions.

The most common purpose of these organizations is maintaining or improving the conditions of employment.

Over the last 300 years, many trade unions have developed into a number of forms, influenced by differing political and economic regimes. The immediate objectives and activities of trade unions vary, but usually include the *provision of benefits to members, collective bargaining, industrial action* and *political activities.*

■ *Benefits* may include an insurance against unemployment, sick leave and old-age pensions. In many developed countries, these functions have been assumed by the state. The provision of professional training and legal advice are important benefits of union membership.

■ *Collective bargaining* takes place when unions negotiate with employers over wages and working conditions.

■ *Industrial action* may take the form of strikes or resistance to lockouts when negotiations are unfruitful.

■ *Political activities include* campaigning and lobbying to promote legislation favorable to the interests of their members.

Partnership and industry associations

According to the Millennium Development goals (a set of eight goals to be achieved by 2015 that respond to the world's main development challenges including education, health, and environment), cross-sector partnerships are encouraged in order to implement practical solutions in regard to sustainable development (UN, 2008). Cross-sector partnerships mean governments, non-governmental organizations, the public and private sector as well as local communities working together (Green Hotelier, 2005). In addition, industry members need to work together with each other as well as with other stakeholders in order to break down barriers to progress and better address issues in regard to sustainable practices (Green Hotelier, 2006b). As stated by David Roberts, General Manager of the *Fairmont Chateau Whistler Resort*, 'we all have the power of one' and collectively, 'individuals can move mountains' and 'corporations can make single decisions to shift policy that in time will produce major cultural and behavioural change' (Harris *et al.*, 2002: 269). Working together with other hospitality operations in the area for environmental reasons can improve strategic relationships and help to improve environmental standards (Webster, 2000). Making use of industry associations and schemes often can help implementing sustainable programs and achieve higher standards. International and national certification schemes, such as

Green Globe 21, provide tools and support in regard to sustainable practices for tourism businesses (Green Hotelier, 2007a). Joining organizations such as *Slow Food* also could help a restaurant especially in regard to establishing ties to local producers and obtaining information about regional produce and tastes. In addition, getting involved in associations or partnerships keeps one updated, provides new ideas and enhances the critical view in regard to sustainability. Therefore, participation and engagement in such associations or partnerships can be highly recommended.

CASE STUDY 10.1: Slow Food

Slow Food is a non-profit organization that was founded in 1986 by Carlo Petrini in Italy, and currently has more than 85,000 members in 132 countries (Slow Food, n.d.). 'Slow Food is "good," "clean" and "fair,"' believing that the 'food we eat should taste good; that it should be produced in a clean way that does not harm the environment, animal welfare or our health; and that food producers should receive fair compensation for their work' (Slow Food, n.d., para. 2).

According to Tschirner *et al.* (2007), the organization aims to secure a better future by defending biodiversity in the food supply, promoting taste education and linking sustainable producers with customers. Actions include initiatives such as the development of the 'ark of taste' for each region where culinary traditions and flavors are rediscovered and preserved.

CSR AND COMPANY PERFORMANCE: GREENWASH VERSUS ACCOUNTABILITY

CorpWatch is an organization located in San Francisco dedicated to watch, as its name truly depicts, corporations around the globe. Unethical behavior in corporations is analyzed and widely spread via Internet articles. CorpWatch has put in place a *Greenwash* contest. The awards are given to companies that largely publicize respectable actions undertaken to cover up either environmentally damaging operations or various unscrupulous activities. The food and beverage industry is under tight scrutiny and many large restaurant organizations do not escape independent reviews and critics. Numerous corporations spend more on corporate image advertising that boasts about humanitarian programs than on the programs themselves (be it charities, donations or contributions). This is so-called *Greenwash*. Hence, the troublesome issue is that CSR can easily become just another public relations exercise! Independent organizations often created by various stakeholders are cropping up everywhere, reminding businesses of the need to be accountable for their actions. For many owners and managers, CSR is still driven more by the concern about the negative public relations consequences of ignoring CSR than by the potential benefits of embracing a responsible behavior.

Profits are only one measure of benefits, based on quantitative data. Companies have experienced a range of bottom-line benefits, measured on both quantitative and qualitative data. Table 10.2 depicts the overall benefits from CSR at the business level, supported by short examples or added information.

CSR is synonymous to business success. However, perspectives on business development in regard to short-term gains versus long-term benefits has to be revised to incorporate the issue of sustainable development.

Table 10.2	Corporate Social Responsibility Overall Business Benefits[*]
CSR Benefits	**Example/Explanation**
Improved financial performance	Several academic studies have shown a correlation between CSR and improved financial performance. Through improved innovation, competitiveness and market positioning, CSR is as much about seizing opportunity as avoiding risk. Drawing feedback from diverse stakeholders can be a rich source of ideas for new products, processes and markets, resulting in competitive advantages.
Reduced operating costs	The improved operational efficiency through a systematic approach to management that includes continuous improvement is key in reducing operating costs. *Environmentally oriented program*: Energy efficiency reducing utility bills, recycling reducing waste disposal costs.
	Human Resources program: Work–life scenario reducing absenteeism and increasing retention, thus reducing employee turnover costs.
Enhanced brand image and reputation	Organizations that perform well with regard to CSR can build their reputation. Reputation, or brand equity, is founded on values such as trust, credibility, reliability, quality and consistency.
Responsible consumerism and customer loyalty	Ethical conduct and environmental and social consciousness of companies make a difference in purchasing decisions. Companies have a key role to play in facilitating sustainable consumption patterns and lifestyles through the goods and services they provide and the way they provide them.
Increased productivity and quality	Improved working conditions equal to a greater employee involvement in decision-making processes, increasing productivity and reducing failures.
Increased ability to attract and retain employees	Strong CSR commitment facilitates recruitment of highly qualified candidates, boosts morale and results in higher retention rates. Employees are not only front-line sources of ideas for improved performance, but are champions of a company for which they are proud to work.
Improved relations with regulators	In a number of jurisdictions, governments have expedited approval processes for firms that have undertaken social and environmental activities beyond those required by regulation.
Access to capital	Financial institutions are increasingly incorporating social and environmental criteria into their assessment of projects. When making decisions about where to place their money, investors are looking for indicators of effective CSR management. A business plan incorporating a good CSR approach is often seen as a proxy for good management.

[*]*Adapted from the International Institute for Sustainable Development www.iisd.org*

CSR BUSINESS STRATEGY: INTERNAL ISSUES AND GLOBAL CHALLENGES

Many food and beverage companies have increasingly demonstrated of social management practices and environmental responsibility. So far, a large number of firms have been stuck at the first stage of CSR integration into strategic thinking, that of *pollution prevention* (Hart, 1997) (see Figure 10.3). Some companies have moved to a second stage, which looks not only at pollution in general, but also at the environmental impact of the full product life cycle. Stuart Hart, Director of the Sustainable Enterprise Initiative at the University of Carolina's Business Schools, describes this second stage as *product stewardship* (Hart, 1997). The third level looks at the development of so-called *clean technologies* contributing to the solution of environmental and social challenges (Hart, 1997). These three stages forge a company's way to sustainability. Hart argues that 'a clear and fully integrated environmental strategy should not only guide competency development, it should also shape the company's relationship to customers, suppliers, other companies, policy-makers and all its stakeholders' (Hart, 1997).

Important aspects of a successful CSR program are:

- Clear policies
- Commitment and agreement on objectives
- Resources made available
- No conflicts with other policies
- Coordination of efforts and communication by a committee or problem-solving group

Therefore, one of the first steps toward integrating CSR within the hospitality industry is to develop businesswide policies, recognizing the importance of the business to economic development of regions and the responsibilities

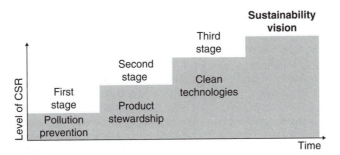

FIGURE 10.3   *Corporate social responsibility integration stages. (Reprinted by permission of Harvard Business Review. From "Beyond Greening: Strategies for a Sustainable World" by Hart, S., 75(1) 1997.) Copyright © 2002 by the Harvard Business School Publishing Corporation; all rights reserved.*

toward the community and the surrounding environment. In short, the policy should cover the following aspects:

- Develop a written policy statement covering all areas

- Incorporate the mission statement

- Be inspired from code of practices as minimum standards

- Set realistic and measurable targets, including key performance targets and periodic audits compatible with trading partners (suppliers). Then, the policy could be transformed into objectives (see Table 10.3) leading to success factors.

Table 10.3	Stakeholders Policies and Expectations	
Stakeholders	**Policy**	**Expectations**
Employees	We shall educate and facilitate for our employees to make a conscious decision in favor of environmental, ethical and social issues in their private and work lives.	Fair and equal treatment; secure and safe working environment; training and career progress; good pay.
Customers	We shall inform and make it easy for our guests to participate in responsible business-related activities at our hotels.	Leading service; good value for money; flexible approach; environmentally responsible; good global coverage; benefits and generous loyalty programs.
Property owners	We shall work together with property owners to find innovative solutions that satisfy our economic, environmental and social objectives.	Good returns from property management; high level of security.
Shareholders	We shall provide shareholders and investors with timely, accurate and transparent information on responsible business-related risks and opportunities.	Transparent information; sound strategy and corporate governance; high return on investment; minimization of risks.
Suppliers	We shall strive to purchase products that have a reduced environmental impact during their life cycle, from suppliers that demonstrate environmental and social responsibility.	Fair and equal treatment; value-based pricing.
Authorities	We require our managers to abide by local and international legislation, especially regarding labor laws, Health and Safety, human rights and the environment.	Compliance with rules and regulations; financial contributions (taxes and fees).
Community	We shall take an active role in the international responsible business community, and contribute to the local communities where we operate.	Forming an active and responsible part of society; sponsorships of projects; contribution to infrastructure; contribution to attractiveness of destination.
Environment	We shall do our utmost to continuously improve our performance in the areas of energy, water, chemicals and resource consumption, and waste generation in order to reduce our negative impact on the environment.	Reduced consumption of energy, water and chemicals; resource-efficiency; biodiversity protection; minimization of waste; responsible purchasing; sustainable transport.

Source: Sustainability Report of The Rezidor Hotel Group (2008).

■ Translate success factors into goals which in turn should convert to activities (see Table 10.4).

Table 10.4	Stakeholders Objectives, Indicators, Targets and Achievements			
Responsible Business Policy	**Responsible Business Objectives (Example)**	**Responsible Business Indicators (Example)**	**Commitments and Targets for 2008 (Example)**	**Achievements 2008 (Example)**
Employees	Increase employee awareness regarding responsible business.	Number of hotels and employees with responsible business training.	Launch new suite of training 'Living Responsible Business' and 'Leading Responsible Business'.	New Responsible Business Training launched at the Business School in July 2008.
Customers	Provide responsible business actions that are easy for guests to participate in.	Number of measures to help guests save energy and water consumption and reduce waste generation.	Put in place more measures that encourage guests to participate in waste reduction and sorting.	78% of hotels make battery collection box available for guests; 93% of hotels provide refillable amenity dispensers in public washrooms.
Property owners	Inform all property owners about the responsible business program to facilitate the use of best responsible business practice when building and renovating.	Number of hotel owners informed about program and local Responsible Business Action Plan.	Inform owners of at least 90% of the hotels about the responsible business program and local responsible business action plan.	87% hotel owners informed about programme and local responsible business action plan.
Shareholders	All hotels to comply with the reporting requirements of the responsible business program.	Percentage of hotels that report quarterly and annually to corporate office.	Maintain high reporting level from managed and leased hotels (100%).	100% of managed and leased hotels responded to two sets of mandatory reports.
Suppliers	Increase the number of products purchased that comply with set responsible business criteria for product group.	Number of corporate communication items printed on recycled/eco-labeled paper.	Use recycled paper for corporate responsible business communication material.	100% of responsible business communication items printed on recycled paper.
		Number of energy and water saving devices in hotels.	Increase the number of energy and water saving devices in hotels.	64% of hotels have occupancy sensors/motion detectors/timers to control lightning in intermittent use areas.
Authorities	Zero number of incidents of non-compliance with regard to responsible business-related legislative demands and international agreements.	Percentage of hotels performing responsible business legal self-audit.	100% of hotels to perform self-audit where available.	97% of hotels perform legal-self-audit where available.

Source: Sustainability Report of The Rezidor Hotel Group (2008).

A company undergoing transformation to incorporate CSR issues must revise internal practices regarding *governance, core ideology, organizational alignment, audits and accounting practices* as well as *education for social responsibility*. These practices contribute effectively to CSR in the following ways:

Governance is about the planning, influencing and conducting of the policy and monitoring the long-term strategy and direction of the business.

Core ideology defines the values a company espouses, describing a sense of purpose well beyond profit or shareholders' wealth maximization. It was found that visionary companies 'tended to pursue a cluster of objectives, of which making money is only one – and not necessarily the primary one' (Collins and Porras, 2001). Core ideologies have very limited benefits if not translated into actions and 'ensured that they are reflected consistently throughout the organisation in everything the company does' (Palazzi and Starcher, 2001). Day-to-day decisions, human resource policies, organizational physical environment (buildings, layouts) are only a few areas where organizational alignment to the core ideologies is achieved.

Organizational alignment occurs when all departments within a company understand and work toward the same vision, goals and objectives.

Traditional *audits* are formal examinations of the company's financial situation and accounting practices. Environmental and social audits report how a firm has preformed in terms of its specific CSR objectives or action programs. It is very much like the sub listing of financial results, which may be compared financial forecasts.

Finally, a critical element lies in *education for social responsibility*. In order to integrate responsible business practices into day-to-day operations, the involvement, commitment and knowledge of employees, from the general manager to the front-line server, are essential. Spreading the word about the crucial importance of revising business management techniques is the key to the adoption of CSR behavior.

CHAPTER QUESTIONS

1. Map out who the key internal and external stakeholders are for a hotel or restaurant and identify their potential impacts on the business and wider communities.

2. What are the key responsibilities a hotel or restaurant should take when embracing Corporate Social Responsibility?

3. What are the dangers associated with a hotel or restaurant business undertaking *greenwash* campaigns?

READING LIST

Boulding, K.E., 1966. The economics of the coming spaceship earth. In: Jarrett, H. (Ed.), Environmental Quality in a Growing Economy. Resources for the Future/ Johns Hopkins University Press, Baltimore, MD, pp. 3–14.

Brown, L., 2001. Eco-Economy: Building an Economy for the Earth. W.W. Norton & Company, New York.

Collins, J.C., Porras, J.I., 2001. Built to Last: Successful Habits of Visionary. Companies. Harper Business Essentials, New York.

Green Hotelier, 2000. Corporate social awareness. Green Hotelier 19, 10–11.

Green Hotelier, 2005. Tourism today – how the agenda has evolved. Green Hotelier 36, 6–15.

Green Hotelier, 2006a. Sustainable supply chains. Green Hotelier 38, 1–4.

Green Hotelier, 2006b. The power of partnerships. Green Hotelier 41, 12–19.

Green Hotelier, 2006c. Environmental awareness and training. Green Hotelier 41, 1–4.

Green Hotelier, 2007a. What does it mean to be a sustainable hotel? Green Hotelier 44, 24–26.

Green Hotelier, 2007b. Greening the urban jungle. Green Hotelier 43, 12–18.

Harris, R., Griffin, T., Williams, P., 2002. Sustainable Tourism: A Global Perspective. Butterworth-Heinemann, Oxford.

Hart, S., 1997. Beyond Greening: Strategies for a Sustainable World. Harvard Business Review 75 (1), 66–76.

Martin, R.L., 2002. The virtue matrix: calculating the return on corporate responsibility. Harvard Business Review 80 (3), 68–75.

Omann, I., Spangenberg, J.H., 2002. Assessing social sustainability: the social dimension of sustainability in a socio-economic scenario. In: Proc. 7th Biennial Conference of the International Society for Ecological Economics, March 6–9, Sousse, Tunisia.

Palazzi, M., Starcher, G., 2001. Corporate Social Responsibility and Business Success. European Bahá'I Business Forum, Paris.

Tschirner, M., Rosenbaum, U., Geisel, O., 2007. 15 Jahre Slow Food Deutschland e.V. Convivien, Arche, Schulgarten, Kinder, Events, Internationales, Studieren. Slow Food Deutschland e.V., Ludwigsburg.

United Nations, 2008. The millennium development goals report. United Nations, New York. Available at http://www.un.org/millenniumgoals/pdf/The%20Millenn ium%20Development%20Goals%20Report%202008.pdf.

Webster, K., 2000. Environmental management in the hospitality industry. Cassell, New York.

Welford, R., Starkey, R. (Eds.), 2001. The Earthscan Reader in Business and Sustainable Development. Earthscan Publications, London.

CHAPTER 11

Communicating Environmentally Sustainable Initiatives

<table>
<tr><td>

Study Objectives

- To know the ways of benchmarking sustainable practices
- To understand the initiatives reporting sustainable practices
- To define certification
- To understand the certification procedure and the major benefits associated with certification
- To examine the basic concept surrounding Environmental Management Systems
- To provide a listing of the major international and national eco-labels
- To discern current situation between SMEs and large hotel corporations

</td></tr>
</table>

CONTENTS

A factor of differentiation for hotels and restaurants is the way they communicate their environmental commitment. For many hospitality entrepreneurs, the reduction of environmental impacts and the increase in societal involvement is the credo for successful business management. However, the level of implication in this new approach to business management depends highly on the hotel brands and the type of ownership. Indeed, the implementation of environmental charters is often the responsibility of individual hotel or restaurant directors, who may have other priorities in mind. One of the main objectives sought by implementing environmental and societal initiatives is, besides the observance of legislation, the potential reduction in operating costs. Additionally, good environmental communication can become an advantageous differentiation factor and create a positive brand image.

It is becoming clear from the demand of stakeholders that the hospitality industry needs to communicate effectively on their environmental and social commitment in addition to their economic prosperity. Mandatory reporting is only required for financial information and where products or services are hazardous, which is not generally the case for the hospitality industry. The communication of sustainability efforts or results, however, is far from being as regulated. A large diversity can be noted with regard to the way environmental and social justice information is disseminated and the reasons for its publication. However, the reporting of environmentally sustainable efforts is essential to attract capital from block investors with specific investment guidelines, like the Dow Jones Sustainability Index.

Three ways of communication are described in this chapter:

■ Benchmarking
■ Certification
■ Reporting

The last two can be considered as marketing tools, but reporting to a lesser extent than certification. Certification is often considered to be a communication effort from the company to potential customers voluntarily advertising the company's adherence to certain standards. Benchmarking is more concerned with publishing detailed information accounting for a company's individual efforts to a wider range of stakeholders.

SUSTAINABILITY BENCHMARKING

Benchmarking is a process that is increasingly being incorporated into environmental certification. The main aim of benchmarking is to compare operational efficiency and environmental impact within facilities having a similar portfolio and to indicate possible improvements in business activity, processes and management by establishing more efficient operational standards. Benchmarking is either internal between different departments or sections or external and compares performance data with other organizations at different levels. This comparison can be either between environmental items such as energy, waste and water consumption or social initiatives such as employee satisfaction or participation in local charity events. Benchmarking typically involves the comparison of processes within one's own business and those in other businesses. The development of measures aimed at closing performance gaps are then identified and put into action. Two examples of sustainable benchmarking are Benchmark Hotel Green and Globe 21.

CASE STUDY 11.1: The Sustainability Performance Operation Tool (Spot)

The Sustainability Performance Operation Tool (SPOT) developed by the International Tourism Partnership is a sustainability check instrument for business operations. SPOT graphically demonstrates the sustainability of an operation pertaining to the three pillars: (1) environmental, (2) social and (3) economic, which can be used either as a management information tool or as part of a training process. SPOT structures key principles and indicators of sustainability into a robust framework, from which an appraisal of performance can be undertaken and reported against.

By setting objectives and targets for the coming years and monitoring and reviewing the performance, the SPOT tool contributes to a property's balanced score card system. It also sets standards for a company award-based system using third-party validation. Lastly, SPOT compiles a Corporate Social Responsibility Impact assessment.

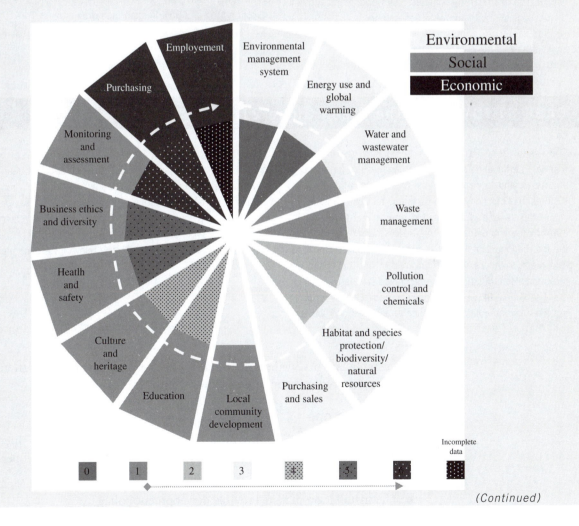

(Continued)

CASE STUDY 11.1: (Continued)

The methodology is easy to use and fully adaptable to all types of operations.

1. Assessment by online questionnaire

The assessment allows optimization of the key elements of sustainability: environmental, social and economic.

2. Results presented dynamically

The results for each set of questions are instantly incorporated into the SPOT chart showing performance at a glance. The chart can be completed by working on each set of questions to obtain an overall assessment.

Tabular reports compare the individual property's scores against those of the company/chain.

3. Customizable reporting

Corporate-level users are able to directly compare their properties' data within their chain/organization. By creating custom made reports and comparisons (e.g. by sector, region or property type), SPOT can be used as a powerful and effective tool that compares options that help strategic operation decision making.

4. Data export

The SPOT charts can be added to documents and presentations. Results can be saved in table format as PDF files using the tool's built-in export feature.

Source: International Tourism Partnership (www.tourismpartnership .org)

CASE STUDY 11.2: The Green Globe 21

The Green Globe 21 (GG21) scheme is a global benchmarking, certification and improvement system for sustainable travel and tourism. It is one of the first self-regulation systems and currently the most widely recognized initiative within the travel and tourism industry. It was launched in 1994 by the World Tourism and Travel Council (WTTC) and the International Hotel and Restaurant Association (IH&RA) as a result of the 1992 Earth Summit in Rio. It is based on the principles of Agenda 21 and ISO-type standards.

The Green Globe 21 initiative is dedicated to improving the environmental performance of all travel and tourism

companies, regardless of size, sector, location or level of environmental activity. Green Globe 21 uses a series of quantitative indicators to benchmark the key aspects of environmental and social performance of an enterprise in all sectors of the travel and tourism industry. The results of indicators for a particular type, activity, market and location of a hospitality operation are compared with the relevant baseline and best-practice levels.

Source: http://www.ec3global.com/

For establishments wishing to achieve Green Globe certification, there is a two-step procedure they must follow.

Phase number one

Phase number one is benchmarking, which lasts approximately three months. It is basically an evaluation of the environmental and societal performance of the hotel. Eight indicators are examined:

- The installation of a sustainable development policy
- Water consumption

- Energy consumption
- Waste management
- Paper consumption
- Pesticide usage
- Maintenance and cleaning products usage
- Engagement with local communities.

The hotel is then benchmarked according to its performance.

Phase number two

Phase number two is certification, which lasts approximately seven months. The hotel management team is required to install an action plan based on good practices. This includes, for example, following legal requirements, water and energy management, management of waste and the management of chemicals. Furthermore, all hotel employees must be implicated in the process and required training procedures. An external and independent auditor reviews the progress. Auditing take place yearly, with visits on property every two years. The hotel is certified if it is in conformity with the requirements of the standard Green Globe.

SUSTAINABILITY REPORTING

Traditionally, businesses and, particularly, the hospitality industry published very little 'nonfinancial' information. With growing pressure from environmental lobby groups and other stakeholders in recent years for more transparency, a lot of companies have started to provide some environmental and social information. *Agenda 21*, signed by 178 member countries of the United Nations, also requested businesses to report on their environmental performance records.

With growing recognition of concepts such as sustainable development, the carbon footprint and the triple bottom line, environmental reporting began to evolve into *corporate social responsibility* (CSR) reporting. The Shell Company was one of the first to highlight the three areas of responsibility – financial, social and environmental. Triple bottom line reporting, or sustainability reporting as it came to be known, thus means to expand traditional reporting on the financial dimension to provide information on environmental and social dimensions also, giving a more balanced view of the overall corporate performance.

As will be seen in the next chapter, many companies from all sections of industry including hospitality now publish stand-alone sustainability reports. Standards of sustainable reporting have started to emerge, although little legislation exists. A major contribution to sustainable reporting was made by the *Global Reporting Initiative* (GRI) in 2002, launching globally applicable sustainability reporting guidelines and performance indicators. These guidelines aim to facilitate reporting on economic, environmental and social performance for corporations, governments and NGOs.

Companies need to keep a large diversity of stakeholders up-to-date about their performance. Primary stakeholders, including shareholders, customers, personnel and suppliers, play an active role in the survival of the company and secondary stakeholders affect and are affected by the company but are not considered to be essential for the survival of the company. However, secondary stakeholders such as the media and non-governmental organizations have a considerable influence on the content and presentation of sustainable reporting.

For example, shareholders have to be informed about company performance and earnings and governmental authorities about tax obligations. For legal reasons, as well as voluntarily, companies publish financial data in balance sheets, income statements and cash flow statements. Besides this external function, reporting also serves as an internal communication and management tool. The most important reasons for publishing sustainability reports, with the exception of financial reports, are still public relations and reputation management. Some companies actually do more in the area of sustainability than they openly communicate.

FOUR CS OF SUSTAINABLE REPORTING

All sustainable reports should incorporate the four Cs of credible reporting:

1. Clear presentation: the report should be user friendly, illustrating programs and results with tables, figures and graphs.

2. Comprehensive coverage: the report should address all issues that are relevant to the company. Addressing only a few issues will send a positive signal to those stakeholders involved in these issues but a negative signal to those involved in other, unaddressed, issues.

3. Consistent inclusion: to enable the comparison of results, reports should address the same issues over time.

4. Comparable measurement and reporting techniques: increases the reliability of the reported progress.

The same problem exists with both reporting and certification, namely the sheer volume of different types and the lack of international standards. Some countries have independently developed legal requirements for environmental reporting, for example, Holland, Sweden, Denmark, the United States and Japan, while others encourage voluntary disclosure. A European effort toward integration and standardization is made by the Eco-Management and Audit Scheme (EMAS). This scheme is a management tool that companies use for evaluation, reporting and improvement purposes. The reliability of the information provided is recognized by the EMAS logo.

EMAS has several requirements that must be fulfilled by organizations that register.

1. Establish an environmental policy

2. External review of the environmental policy by certified consultants

3. Define clear environmental protection objectives following the review

4. Audit all areas related to the policy (waste, water, energy etc.) on a regular basis

REPORTING GUIDELINES AND INDICATORS

To assist companies in the creation of their sustainability reporting, several organizations have developed guidelines and indicators. In the Dow Jones Sustainability Index (DJSI), separate from the Dow Jones World Index, companies are listed that figure in the top 10 concerning the level of sustainability of each industry group. Institutional investors such as pension funds that have started to shift toward adopting environmental and social investment policies increasingly use the DJSI. Selection for this index is based on a questionnaire, which has to be completed by the company. A defined set of criteria and weightings is used to assess the opportunities and risks deriving from economic, environmental and social activities of the eligible companies. Further screening is made of the company and third-party documents as well as personal contacts between the analysts and companies. An external review ensures that the corporate sustainability assessments are completed in accordance with the defined rules.

More precise indicators are proposed by the Global Reporting Initiative (GRI), a collaboration center of the United Nations Environment Programme. In its sustainability reporting guidelines, 35 different indicators are proposed to assess a company's sustainability effort. These indicators are classified in several domains: materials, energy, water, biodiversity, emissions, effluents and waste, suppliers, products and services, compliance, transport and overall performance.

Furthermore, sector supplements are available for several different industry sectors; unfortunately, no separate sector supplement has been created for hospitality operations. The main strength of the GRI indicators is that they are very detailed, although this also creates its weakness: the large number of indicators, which can put off management. Other indicators have been sought at other international CSR certificate institutes, namely the Institute of Social and Ethical Accountability who have created the AA1000 series. This set of corporate responsibility standards is an open-source framework for organizational accountability developed through a multi-stakeholder consultation and review process. These standards are designed to be compatible with other key standards in the area of sustainable development, including the GRI guidelines. As the verification of sustainability reports is not compulsory, unlike the verification of financial reports, the management has still a large degree of control over the verification process, the selection of the auditor, the actual contents and the confidentiality of the auditor's report.

CERTIFICATION: A DEFINITION

Certification is a procedure by which a third party, the certifier, provides a written insurance that a system, a process, a person, a product or a service conform to the requirements specified in a standard or a reference frame. Certification is a voluntary act. It is a tool of competitiveness and differentiation, which establishes consumer confidence.

CERTIFICATION AND QUALITY

Certification and quality are often perceived as being complimentary. This is in part due to the fact that certification recognizes that a company has made or is making effort toward higher-quality levels. It is important to note that the implementation of processes toward higher quality is not always related to the search for certification. Likewise, obtaining certification is not inevitably a pledge for the quality of the products or services offered by the company. Certification is a stamp of approval noting that a business is in conformity with the specified requirements dictated by the certifier.

CONCEPT OF ECO-LABEL

Eco-labels are basically a brand placed on a product, service or organization. The basic goal of an eco-label is to allow the consumer to choose the product, service or company that is recognized to be the most environmentally involved. Eco-labels are voluntary schemes open to all businesses.

DEVELOPMENT OF ECO-LABELS IN THE HOSPITALITY INDUSTRY

In the beginning of the eighties, many manufacturing companies discovered eco-labels as an excellent tool to promote their sustainable efforts. However, in service industries, this development is newer. The lodging industry does not produce, make or grow any products in the traditional sense. Nevertheless, hospitality firms consume natural resources and products on a large scale. Specifically, hotel consumption includes:

- Land
- Construction materials (carpet, paint, wood)
- Fixtures and furnishings
- Cleaning supplies
- Food and beverages
- Technical equipment (air conditioners, computers, elevators, furnaces)
- Energy and water

Eco-labels assess hotels regarding their environmentally sound performance in the above-mentioned areas. After having reached all required benchmarks, the hotel is awarded the particular logo of the eco-label organization and can use this to promote its environmental efforts.

Eco-labels in hospitality have three key functions:

1. Standard setting
2. Certification
3. Marketing

TRENDS IN ECO-LABELING

The trend toward environmental certification, or eco-labeling as it is commonly known, has increased greatly in the last 20 years, primarily because it is an important promotional tool for sustainable tourism and hospitality. In all, eco-labels have three key functions for organizations: environmental standard setting, third-party certification of these standards and value-added marketing or environmental communication. To qualify for an eco-label, hotels have to reach a set environmental standards. The actual certification process makes sure that all required criteria are met before a hospitality company is awarded the eco-label.

However, with the sheer quantity of various eco-labels on the market, the hotel or restaurant guest may struggle to identify which labels are valuable and credible and which are not. The tourism and hospitality industries can choose between over 100 eco-labels worldwide and over 60 just in Europe. It is claimed by industry observers that few hotels use their labels as a marketing tool even when environmentally certified. The problem being that the public and industry are confused by the message the labels are designed to convey. The Voluntary Initiatives for Sustainability in Tourism (VISIT) was set to overcome this confusion, whereby various eco-labels are promoted via VISIT when they meet a particular requirement level. An advisory board including the United Nation Environmental Programme (UNEP), the World Tourism Organization (WTO) and the European Hotel and Restaurant Association (HOTREC), to name a few, supports VISIT.

The labels are often too expensive for individual hotels especially when cost/benefits are not properly understood. They also tend to attract customers interested in ecotourism and have limited marketing power. Lastly, there is a risk that with the existence of such a large number of certificates, companies will choose those that are the least demanding. In some unfortunate circumstances, some establishments have used the lax-control mechanisms associated with some eco-labels to make fraudulent claims. Consequently, consumer recognition is very low. Therefore, the goal envisaged by eco-label certification as a sustainability tool has not yet been effectively reached (WTO, 2004). Arguably, local and regional certification programs should be linked to an international accreditation system.

The Green Globe 21 scheme was designed to overcome these difficulties because the label claims to be global. It is interesting to compare the number of companies that are benchmarked or certified under its label with the number

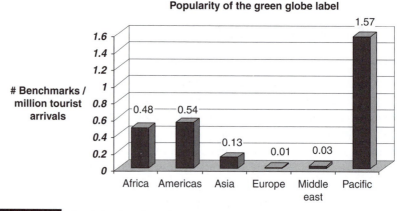

 FIGURE 11.1 *Popularity of the Green Globe Label. Based on Green Globe (2006) and WTO (2005).*

of international tourist arrivals per region. The relatively limited popularity of the Green Globe 21 certification in Europe can be explained by the fact that most of the other certification programs in the travel and tourism industry are European, like ECEAT and Blue Flag, which apparently leaves little market share for Green Globe. Because Green Globe is headquartered in Australia, the label has a striking popularity in the Pacific region. In all, Green Globe cannot be classified as a real global label because its global presence is too small and concentrated. Furthermore, it is interesting to note the low figures for Asia and the Middle East (Figure 11.1).

INTERNATIONAL AND NATIONAL TOURISM- AND HOSPITALITY-RELATED ECO-LABELS

The following is a selection of international and national tourism- and hospitality-related eco-labels (including food-and-beverage-related and other products labels used in hospitality industry, i.e. in sourcing, ingredients etc.).

- The European Eco-label (http://ec.europa.eu/environment/ecolabel/) is labeled as a flower. The label is a voluntary scheme designed to encourage businesses to market products and services that are kinder to the environment and for European consumers to easily identify them. The Flower label covers a wide range of products and service, including tourism accommodation services (to be found at http://www.ecolabel-tourism.eu/).

- The Green Key (http://www.green-key.org/) is the first international environmental label for lodging facilities.

- Green Seal (http://www.greenseal.org/) covers a wide range of products and services and also provides a label to lodging facilities in the United States.

- Green Tourism Business Scheme (http://www.green-business.co.uk/) is the national sustainable tourism certification scheme for the United Kingdom.

- Nordic Swan (http://www.svanen.nu/) is a neutral, independent label, which guarantees a certain environmental standard for a wide variety of products and services, including hotel and restaurant operations. Norway, Sweden, Finland, Iceland and Denmark are participating in the program.

- Viabono (http://www.viabono.de/) is the German eco-label for tourist lodging facilities.

- OE-Plus (http://www.oe-plus.ch/) is an association providing certification for a Swiss label of sustainable development actions.

- Legambiente Turismo (http://www.legambienteturismo.it/) supports the concept of atmosphere and locality in tourism and labels in Italy.

- Ecologo (http://www.ecologo.org/en/) is a Canadian-based third-party certification of environmentally friendly products, including hospitality industry–related products and hotel facilities.

- Good Environmental Choice (http://www.aela.org.au/) is the Australian environmental labeling program, which indicates the environmental performance of a product or service.

- Demeter (http://www.demeter.net/) is an ecological association that has built up a network of individual certification organizations worldwide. The Demeter label is based on biodynamic agricultural methods.

- Blauer Engel (http://www.blauer-engel.de/) is a label dedicated to consumer products in Germany and plays a role in the sourcing and purchasing activities of a hotel or restaurant.

- Eco Mark (http://www.ecomark.jp/english/index.html) is the Japanese scheme on labeling environmentally friendly products, useful in planning the sourcing and purchasing activities in hotels and restaurants.

- Ecomark (http://envfor.nic.in/cpcb/ecomark/ecomark.html) is the Indian scheme on labeling environmentally friendly products, useful in planning the sourcing and purchasing activities of a hotel or restaurant.

- Ecovin (http://www.ecovin.org/) is a German-based organization that encourages organic wine cultivation and production under a set of strict organic agricultural guidelines.

In addition to the labels that are designed specifically for the hospitality, travel and tourism industries, the International Organization for Standardization has developed certifications that do not apply to one industry in particular. ISO 14001 certification is a process-led approach that guides companies through the process of setting up an Environmental Management System (see next chapter). It assesses the attempts of an organization to minimize harmful effects on the environment caused by its activities; it strives to support the company in the continual improvement of its environmental performance. ISO 14001 is becoming more and more popular according to the most recent reports available.

CHAPTER QUESTIONS

1. Choose one eco-label and map out the requirements for a hotel or restaurant to be certified.
2. Identify three challenges and three benefits from implementing an environmental certification within a hotel or restaurant.
3. What are the advantages in setting up an Environmental Management System within a hospitality property?

READING LIST

Bendell, J., Font, X., 2004. Which tourism rules? Green standards and GATS. Ann. Tourism Res. 31 (1), 139–156.

Eco-Management and Audit Scheme, 2009. Guidance documents. European Commission Environment DG, Brussels. Available at http://ec.europa.eu/environment/emas/documents/guidance_en.htm

Font, X., 2002. Environmental certification in tourism and hospitality: progress, process and prospects. Tourism Manag. 23 (3), 197–205.

Font, X., Buckley, R. (Eds.), 2001. Tourism Ecolabelling: Certification and Promotion of Sustainable Management. CABI Publishing, Wallingford, UK.

Green Hotelier., 2002. Environmental labels and certification schemes. Green Hotelier 25–26, 12–19.

Green Hotelier., 2003. Common standards for ecolabels. Green Hotelier 29, 6.

Honey, M. (Ed.), 2002. Ecotourism and Certification: Setting Standards in Practice. Island Press, Washington, DC.

International Standard Organization, 2009. ISO and the Environment. International Standard Organization, Geneva Available at http://www.iso.org/iso/iso_catalogue/management_standards/iso_9000_iso_14000/iso_and_the_environment.htm

International Tourism Partnership. <http://www.tourismpartnership.org/>

Starkey, R., 1999. The standardization of environmental management systems: ISO 14001, ISO 14004 and EMAS. In: Welford, R. (Ed.), Corporate Environmental Management. Earthscan Publications Ltd, London, pp. 61–89.

CHAPTER 12

Hospitality Industry Environmental Management Systems and Strategies

Study Objectives

- To define Environmental Management Systems (EMS)
- To identify the key benefits in establishing an EMS
- To review how large hotel companies are working with EMS
- To draw a set of recommendations for a successful implementation of an EMS

ENVIRONMENTAL MANAGEMENT SYSTEMS: DEFINITION AND OBJECTIVES

A corporate Environmental Management System (EMS) embraces both technical and organizational activities aimed at reducing environmentally negative impacts caused by a company's operations. EMS is a management tool that allows a company to be organized so as to control and reduce its environmental impacts. An EMS is also an engagement toward continuous environmental improvement. The main objectives of the EMS are:

- To respect regulation and go beyond the initial objectives set out in the company's environmental policy.

- To prevent pollution wherever possible.

- To control costs via energy and material savings.

- To improve environmental performance even where regulation requirements do not exist.

- To ensure transparent communication toward employees, communities and consumers.

THE BENEFITS OF EMS TO THE COMPANY

The benefits for businesses implementing EMS are manifold, including:

- Image profiling – showing engagement as a responsible business.

- Tool for dialogue – the EMS reinforces partner confidence (consumers, investors, communities, associations and organizations for environmental protections, public authorities etc.).

- Prevention – a possible return on investment in regard to consumption and waste management.

- Internal motivation – the employees join in a project that has direct impact on their professional lives (health, safety).

- Anticipating environmental and sustainable development trends – the rise in awareness of the concept of sustainable development allows companies having anticipated environmental protection development to profit from a first-mover advantage.

- Marketing – a positive image of a caring, environment-friendly organization can be developed and can be used to differentiate itself from the competition.

Any management action or set of actions that benefit the environment can be called an environmental management system. As it is unlikely that hotel executives have sufficient knowledge to install a set of measures that comprehensively treat all the environmental impacts of their establishment, most companies turn to a recognized environmental standards organization. The standards most commonly used in Europe are the globally valid ISO 14000 series of environmental standards and the EU EMAS directive (eco-audit).

The standards ISO 14001 and ISO 14004 both define the specifications and guidelines for an EMS implementation, while the standards ISO 14010, ISO 14011 and ISO 14012 define the principles and procedures of environmental audits, as well as the qualification criteria of the auditors. Both EMAS and ISO require each operational unit to produce a fully documented environmental program. Responsibilities for the staff are defined and environmental objectives with delays are agreed. An independent expert verifies compliance with all the regulations and the implementation of the environmental objectives.

CASE STUDY 12.1: Accor Hotels

Accor's annual report 2005 (Accor, 2006) can be classified as a real sustainability report. The company reports strategies, specific actions, quantified objectives and results. Sixteen pages, or 14%, of the annual report is dedicated to the elaboration of sustainable strategies, in environmental as well as social and economic domains. The recognition for Accor's efforts is demonstrated by the inclusion of the company in the Dow Jones Sustainability Index, FTSE4Good Europe, Ethibel Sustainability Index and ASPI Eurozone.

The goals of their 'Earth Guest' program, launched in 2006, are: to reduce water and energy consumption, promote balanced nutrition and double in three years the number of hotels that propose fair-trade products. The program is divided into two parts: a social responsibility development area (EGO) and an environmental responsibility development area (ECO).

Accor counts among the biggest hotel chains and currently manages 4,121 hotels under 13 different brands worldwide (*Sofitel, Pullman, Novotel, Mercure, Suitehotel, Adagio, Ibis, All Seasons, Etap, Formule 1, Motel 6, Studio 6, Accor Thalassa*) (Accorhotels 2007). Accor claims to be one of the first hotel chains to have implemented a comprehensive global environmental policy. In 1994, Accor set up an environmental department exclusively responsible to generate a creative environmentally sustainable business approach. This department now consists of 56 correspondents worldwide and is led by one designated environmental manager. The environmental policy is made up of eight key projects (Accor 2007):

1. Principles of Action
2. Hotelier's Environment Charter
3. Water and Energy
4. Waste Traceability
5. Eco-labels and Sustainable Purchasing
6. Building Construction
7. Customer Awareness and Information
8. Environmental Certification

Principles of Action comprises nine rules and determines the way all environmental actions should be carried out. The second project, Hotelier's Environmental Charter, is Accor's internal benchmarking tool and provides the local hotel managers with guidelines for environmentally sustainable business practices. It gives hotel managers and employees clear instructions on how resources can be saved in the areas of energy, water and waste. Moreover, it explains how guests should be approached regarding environmental issues. Additionally, the 'Environment Charter' gives information on topics like the ozone layer, biodiversity and sustainable procurement. According to Accor's annual report 2006, 3,228 of the 4,121 hotels are acting according to the 'Environmental Charter' (Accor Annual Report 2006). Since its introduction seven years ago, this 68-page informational tool has played a vital role in internal information and communication.

The third point Accor's environmental policy considers is energy and water. Apart from mentioning the importance of improving energy and water efficiency, Accor is taking a very proactive approach in regard to renewable energy. In 2003, Accor set up 19 solar panels across its hotels and has used the generated energy for hot water production. This measure saves 328 tons of carbon dioxide annually and generates between 40 and 60% of the individual hotels' hot water consumption. Meanwhile, the solar panel project has been extended to an additional 20 hotels, especially on the African continent where efficiency is particularly high. Waste Traceability chiefly concerns the separation of waste, where the company already achieves a high score in France owing to its proactive information policy (Accor 2007). The fifth pillar of Accor's environmental policy refers to Eco-labels and Sustainable Purchasing.

According to their web page, Accor prefers eco-labeled suppliers. In 2002, Accor dispatched an environmental purchasing charter to its purchasing organizations as well as to over 2,000 preferred suppliers. This charter requests the sustainability of food and nonfood products. After collecting and processing the information from its suppliers, Accor sent out reports that specify areas in which suppliers

(Continued)

CASE STUDY 12.1: (Continued)

can improve their performance. In sustainable construction, Accor cooperates with the French 'Haute Qualité Environnementale,' standard for sustainable buildings. This approach has been implemented in one Novotel in Paris.

The last point in Accor's environmental policy is Environmental Certification. Accor claims that it operates more hotels with environmental certification than any other hotel chain. To date, approximately 10 Accor hotels have been certified with ISO 14001. Additionally, 16 other Accor

hotels have been certified by other certification organizations. Besides the eight key topics, Accor actively engages in several humanitarian projects as well as in initiatives to fight child sex tourism. In credit to Accor, the company has designated an extra section on environmental sustainability in its annual report. Shareholders are informed about environmental programs as well as achievements.

Source: Accor Annual Report 2006

CASE STUDY 12.2: InterContinental Hotels Group

With over 4000 hotels globally, the InterContinental Hotels Group (IHG) have a large responsibility and a unique opportunity to make a positive difference. In 2008, the IHG completed a detailed carbon footprint analysis and measured energy, water and waste in IHG's owned and managed hotels. Carbon footprinting is a developing area whereby the carbon footprint is measured by undertaking a GHG (greenhouse gas) emissions assessment including direct and indirect emissions arising from items such as materials, waste, water and transport use and helps to identify the hot-spots in terms of energy consumption and associated CO2-emissions. The research estimated the IHG's carbon dioxide emissions are 9 million tonnes each year or approximately 63,000 return flights from London to Miami. Given that IHG is a hotel

company, it is sensible to break this number down into a per room night figure and compare this performance against that of IHG guests in their own homes.

In this analysis IHG found that the average hotel footprint is approximately equal to the average US family staying at home. On a per room night sold basis, IHG's carbon footprint average is 59kgs. At the best performing hotels in the study, the carbon footprint was significantly lower (22kgs) than staying at home (average US home).

With this understanding, IHG can set a carbon objective that is more tangible than a straight percentage target.

Source: InterContinental Hotels Group (www. ihgplc.com)

CASE STUDY 12.3: Marriott Hotels and Resorts

Marriott Hotels and Resorts operates 2,832 hotels spread across 13 different brands, covering all segments ranging from the three-star Courtyard by Marriott to five-star luxury brands like the JW or Ritz-Carlton (Marriott Hotels and Resorts 2007).

Marriott Hotels and Resorts is still the only hotel group that is a partner of Energy Star, the US environmental government program that assesses companies, products and services according to their energy efficiency. In 2006, Marriott was named 'Partner of the Year' for implementing

(Continued)

CASE STUDY 12.3: (Continued)

programs that save 86 million kilowatt-hours of electricity and as a consequence 68,000 tons of greenhouse gas. At present, 250 Marriott Hotels are awarded with the Energy Star label (Marriott Hotels and Resorts 2007).

Marriott has a companywide environmental program in place called 'Environmentally Conscious Hospitality Operations' (ECHO), with the purpose of providing guidance to all Marriott Hotels (Marriott Hotels and Resorts 2007) and works in the following areas:

- Water and energy conservation
- Clean-air initiatives (all hotels in the United States and Canada are nonsmoking)
- Reduce-reuse-recycle programs
- Cleanup campaigns
- Wildlife preservation

Marriott encourages environmental cleaning initiatives, where its employees clean up parks and care for wildlife. The company fosters relationships with local communities, which it regards as important resources.

Marriott has set itself a challenging goal by aiming to reduce carbon dioxide emissions between 2000 and 2010 by one-fifth (1 million tons) (Marriott Hotels and Resorts 2007). This significant reduction clearly shows the aspiration of Marriott to work toward more sustainable operations.

CASE STUDY 12.4: Hilton Hotels Corporation

Hilton's declared mission is '...to ultimately become the industry leader in environmental management...' (Hilton We Care 2007). The Hilton Company comprises 2,935 hotels and has a separate Web site on environmental issues namely www.hiltonwecare.com. Similar to Marriott, Hilton has chosen to focus its efforts on four specific areas: energy efficiency, waste reduction, water efficiency and chemical use reduction in the Hilton Environmental Reporting (HER) system (Hilton We Care 2004). The HER system allows immediate transfer of worldwide environmental data to facilitate regular reporting on Hilton's environmental performance and impacts. The system shares environmental data on particular properties between all stakeholders, from technical experts to area managers. This approach supports Hilton's internal benchmarking process on a property by property basis and gathers information about overall corporate environmental impacts (Hilton Worldwide 2007).

First and foremost, Hilton focuses on motivating its own employees to change their mind-sets toward more sustainable operations before involving guests. Hilton requests its staff members to actively participate in the eco-learning program of the Hilton University. This e-learning tool can be accessed by all Hilton staff members and aims at enhancing environmental awareness and knowledge. Furthermore, Hilton offers its employees the possibility to make suggestions for improvements. A downloadable form on the 'We Care' Web site asks the employees to propose environmental initiatives. Ideas are then evaluated and discussed by the 'We Care' team. In addition, posters and environmental pocketguides are distributed to local staff. The 'We Care' program is limited to Europe and Africa.

The key pillars of the 'We Care' program (Hilton We Care 2007) are:

1. Staff involvement and internal motivation
2. CEO support
3. Internal competition
4. Data measurement tools
5. Centralized data evaluation

CASE STUDY 12.5: Starwood Hotels and Resorts Worldwide Inc.

Starwood Hotels and Resorts Worldwide Inc. (871 hotels). The Starwood business model includes the ownership, management and franchising of hotels, resorts, spas, residences and vacation ownership properties under nine different brands: *Sheraton, Four Points by Sheraton, ALoft, W Hotels, Le Meridien, The Luxury Collection, Westin, Element* and *St. Regis*. Starwood's product portfolio focuses on the high end market. Information about Starwood's environmental programs is scarce. Starwood pursues a very broad approach in terms of sustainable management. For example, it has a program in place called 'Check out for Children,' which raises money for UNICEF's immunization program, thus supporting the health of children in developing countries. Additionally, Starwood supports an educational program called 'Youth Career Initiative' for young people from disadvantaged backgrounds. Starwood has introduced an environmental awareness raising program in Europe, the Middle East and Africa.

A so-called energy toolkit and training program has been distributed to Starwood departmental heads. It contains simple but effective advice about possibilities to save energy in each hotel department. Starwood has implemented fuel cells, which extract hydrogen from natural gas and convert it into electricity and usable waste heat. The Starwood Capital Group is planning to introduce the world's first luxury, eco-friendly hotel brand simply called '1.' All hotels will be built from scratch using environmentally sustainable architecture and interior design. The first five hotels will be built up in the United States using environmentally sustainable building material. Each property will be built according to LEED (Leadership in Energy and Environmental Design) standards. Also, it is planned that each property donates 1% of its revenues to the local community for development purposes.

CASE STUDY 12.6: Fairmont Hotels & Resorts

Fairmont Hotels & Resorts is one of the largest luxury hotel companies in North America. Their portfolio consists of 50 hotels and resorts, located in Canada, the United States, Mexico, Bermuda, Barbados, the United Kingdom, Monaco and the United Arab Emirates. Besides their reputation of excellent service, Fairmont Hotels & Resorts is one of the main actors in the sustainable development of the hospitality industry. In the 1990s, they developed the Green Partnership Program, on the basis of their belief that 'The environment isn't just something that's "out there"– it's where we live, work and play each day' (Fairmont). Several projects were developed in cooperation with the Environmental Media Association (EMA), which connects mass media, the environmental community and consumers. The introduction of the 'Eco-Innovation' Program focuses on giving the employees a key role in the process of developing and implementing new ideas. The program targets the hotel-based environment and connects local initiatives in order to achieve the global

target of sustainable development. Examples of their activities are the employee's development of recycling giveaways, effective waste prevention and eco-friendly catering. Owing to the suggestions of the employees, 20 projects will be implemented each year. After each season, the results will be checked in regard to their efficiency. One of their projects is the 'Green Meeting' Program. It includes suggestions for coffee breaks during meetings. By booking a Green Meeting, the Fairmont hotel will restrict its offers to organic food and Fair Trade Coffee. One of the chain's main targets is to purchase as much local food as possible and to use local resources. Cooperation with the local farmers was created, as it is of major importance for Fairmont Hotels & Resorts, so that the hotel's benefit will not be limited to the guests alone but are spread to the local population as well. Fairmont Hotels & Resorts is an example for the combination of luxury hospitality and sustainable development with a profit for both parties.

CASE STUDY 12.7: Small Hotel Initiatives Bring Awards

The Miami Hotel is an 80 room establishment located in West Melbourne, Australia, catering to the budget-conscious traveler. The Miami Hotel has been involved in the Savings in the City program from its inception. The City of Melbourne's Savings in the City is an innovative environmental program to help city hotels cut energy, water and waste consumption. The Savings in the City program provides leadership, support, recognition, toolkits and advice on environmental management.

A key goal of the Miami Hotel is to continue to make improvements in environmental sustainability. The Savings in the City program has been commercially advantageous to the Miami Hotel because guests appreciate knowing that the hotel is trying to do the right thing, especially guests from drought affected areas.

The Miami Hotel has won Tourism Victoria's Standard Accommodation Award three years in a row and was recently inducted into their Hall of Fame. Staff at the Miami received really positive feedback from Tourism Victoria about the sustainability measures they had introduced. Their focus on the environment also helped the Miami Hotel gain its Camping Association accreditation.

WASTE

Staff at the Miami Hotel have always used recycled paper and recycled their toner cartridges. As a result of the waste audit they're now also:

- Asking guests to separate recyclable materials from the waste put in hotel bins.
- Using commingled recycling bins.
- Using a mattress recycling business, to collect and recycle the hotel's old mattresses.

Tracking the savings

The Miami Hotel has achieved a total reduction of 50% in the waste it produces over the last three years.

On average, hotels produce nearly 12 litres of waste per guest night. Miami Hotel has gone from 8.6 to 4.3 litres, making it a leading performer just by applying a few simple initiatives.

The next step

To help reduce the amount of waste produced by their guests during their stay, the Miami Hotel is:

- Asking guests to request less packaging from the shops they visit.
- Considering introducing a recycled "Miami bag" that guests can take shopping.
- Looking at giving organic waste to the local primary school for their worm farm.

WATER

The water audit provided the Miami Hotel with valuable information on a range of water saving practices available to them. Staff at the Miami Hotel discovered that they were already doing a lot to save water, such as using flow regulators and aerators on taps and shower heads.

The Savings in the City program has encouraged the Miami to:

- Install AAA rated showerheads.
- Mulch gardens at the hotel rather than watering them.
- Install front loading washing machines in the guest laundry which is saving approximately 328 kilometers and $460/yr.

Tracking the savings

Staff at the Miami Hotel were pleasantly surprised to discover they had achieved a 30% reduction in their water use during the Savings in the City project, a saving three times greater than what they had originally anticipated. Hotels using less than 194 litres per guest per night are considered best practice – and the Miami Hotel is going even further by only using 162 litres per guest per night.

The next step

The Miami Hotel has already installed dual flush toilets and is looking at adding restrictors that only flush the toilets while the button is held down. This is expected to save 67 kilolitres and $130 per year.

(Continued)

CASE STUDY 12.7: (Continued)

Staff at the Miami Hotel look forward to installing a water tank but the complexity and cost associated with plumbing into the system has been an issue to date. The Miami Hotel has suggested that assistance for locating funding for major environmental infrastructure could be very useful, particularly for small businesses.

ENERGY

While the Miami Hotel has not yet undertaken an energy audit, because of the enthusiasm generated by the Savings in the City program they have already instituted a number of energy saving measures.

The Miami Hotel has taken a range of actions to reduce energy consumption, including:

- Replacing incandescent light globes throughout the hotel with compact fluorescents.

- Turning off air conditioners when they're not needed.

- Posting notices to guests and staff requesting that they turn off lights when they are not needed.

- Investigating replacing halogen down lighting with LED globes.

Tracking the savings

The Miami Hotel has achieved an impressive one-third reduction in its energy use, from around 80 megajoules per guest per night to less than 50 megajoules. Given that the best practice target is 140 megajoules this is a very impressive result from the Miami Hotel.

Source: City of Melbourne, www.melbourne.vic.gov.au/greenhotels

CASE STUDY 12.8: Green Boutique Hotel

Alto Hotel On Bourke is a boutique hotel located at the western end of Bourke Street in Melbourne, Australia. The Alto Hotel is a purpose built and designed green hotel, incorporating many groundbreaking sustainability measures that may one day become standard for all hotels.

Benefits of Savings in the City

The Alto Hotel on Bourque is participating in the programme Savings in the City – Green Hotels. The program run in the City of Melbourne helps hotels make environmental improvements. The Alto reported that there were substantial cost savings with all the measures they introduced but that,

"The greatest saving is in advertising dollars, the greener you are, the more free press you get - the more good will you generate. It's a very strong calling card and it's amazing how many people respond positively to it."

Alto management reported that while there were financial benefits associated with the savings they have made, the primary reason for introducing wide ranging sustainability

measures was a deep sense of responsibility towards protecting the environment.

WASTE

"We minimise our waste by not supplying throw away plastic toiletries containers, which are usually thrown out half full anyway."

The Alto Hotel on Bourke has developed some great ways to vastly minimise their waste output, including:

- Installing body wash, moisturiser, shampoo and conditioner dispensers in showers rather than using disposable containers. All toiletries used are biodegradable.

- Using dual chamber eco-bins in all rooms where guests can sort their recyclables.

- Processing all organic waste on the premises, the worm castings being used as fertiliser.

(Continued)

CASE STUDY 12.8: (Continued)

- Using recycled paper and toner cartridges in the offices.

- Using recycled toilet paper and facial tissues.

Recycling all their organic waste means that the Alto Hotel on Bourke does not need to use an organic waste service. Using dispensers in the bathrooms means that the hotel also saves on purchasing costs for individual containers.

The staff at Alto are passionate about running a successful and environmentally responsible hotel. Tracking the savings, the Alto Hotel's waste audit and results speak for themselves and their challenge will be to retain these great results over the coming years. They produce only 4.7 litres of waste per guest night, almost half the best practice targets for waste efficiency in hotels.

The next step

The Alto Hotel on Bourke continues to look for new ways to further reduce their waste and look forward to continuing their initiatives with the Savings in the City program.

WATER

The Alto Hotel on Bourke's audits showed that their toilets were flushing on average five times per day, so reducing their cistern capacity has had an enormous impact.

The Alto Hotel on Bourke incorporates a range of water saving techniques, including:

- Aerators on all taps and shower heads.

- Flow restrictors on all taps and showerheads.

- Dual flush AAA rated water efficient toilets.

- Toilet cisterns that use 6 litre full flushes and 3 litre half flushes.

- Push down plugs in bathrooms.

- Conical hand basins that don't require as much water to fill.

- Condenser front loading washing/dryer machines.

- Rain water tanks on the Hotel's roof that provide water for gardening, cleaning out laneways, and carports.

The Alto Hotel on Bourke reported that these investments paid for themselves within the first 22 months of operation. More importantly, they are saving vast amounts of Melbourne's precious drinking water.

Tracking the savings

Alto Hotel on Bourke's water use for its first year of involvement in the Savings in the City program was a mere 119 litres per guest per night, dramatically lower then the 05/06 baseline benchmark of 278 litres and the best practice target of 194 litres.

The next step

Management has recently installed:

- A pump providing rain-water to all public toilet cisterns in dining room and staff rooms.

- New, more effective water-flow-reducers to all taps and showers in the hotel, all taps are down to 5 litres per minute, all showers are down to 8 litres per minute. This should show significant further savings of around 160 litres per day.

ENERGY

"A lot of what we did was more expensive up front but has payed huge dividends now we're operating."

Energy conservation is another area where the Alto Hotel on Bourke excels. Management has introduced a vast array of measures to minimize the hotel's energy consumption:

- Card operated power in all rooms.

- 6-star rated inverter air conditioners that use 40% less power than non-inverter air conditioning.

- "Green tinted" triple glazed windows that absorb UV rays and keep guest rooms cooler.

- Purchasing 100% "Green Power".

- Double insulation wh ich improves sound proofing, and also saves on heating and cooling.

- Windows that can be opened completely to improve air flow and reduce the need for air conditioning.

(Continued)

CASE STUDY 12.8: (Continued)

■ 100% of primary lighting and 70% of secondary lighting uses compact fluorescents.

The Alto Hotel on Bourke reported that while its energy saving measures were more expensive up front, they resulted in huge long-term savings in maintenance and replacement and reduced energy bills.

Tracking the savings
The Alto Hotel on Bourke's energy consumption of 37 megajoules per guest per night is far below the best practice target of 140 megajoules - an amazingly small amount,

demonstrating the benefits of their energy conservation initiatives.

The next step
The Alto Hotel on Bourke has on trial 2 watt LED light globes reading lights, which use 90% less electricity than incandescent light globes and last 22,000 hours longer. If they are successful the Alto Hotel on Bourke will introduce them as reading lights throughout the hotel.

Source: City of Melbourne, www.melbourne.vic.gov.au/greenhotels

CLASSIFICATION OF ENVIRONMENTAL STRATEGIES

Because the publishing of sustainability reports (either concentrating on one of the pillars of sustainability or on a combination) serves public relations (PR) and reputation management–related goals, one can only presume that those companies that do not publish such reports have not yet developed strategies in this domain or have not reached the quantity and quality necessary to satisfy the expectations of their stakeholders.

The differences in the environmental management strategies between the largest companies in the hotel industry with respect to the environment are striking. A few of them can be classified as showing a real proactive behavior. They have programs in place for management, employees and hotel guests. They invest in a range of energy-efficient, water conservation and waste-reduction initiatives and technology. After these *top-of-the-class* companies, there are companies that appear to only care about the damage they inflict upon the environment when they are held legally responsible for it. Furthermore, they seem to be stuck in the old business paradigms that prevent them from seeing the positive effects of sustainable investments on the triple bottom line.

The top-of-the-class hotel chains that are performing very well in the domain of environmental management used to have a real competitive advantage in terms of monetary savings in energy and water costs. However, the issue of environmental degradation has already moved out of its growth phase into a development phase. This means that companies that are actively handling this issue do not have a competitive advantage anymore, but they have eliminated a competitive disadvantage. This competitive disadvantage has not yet been eliminated though by every company in the industry.

RECOMMENDATIONS FOR SUSTAINABILITY

Involve staffs in 'greening' activities

Starting at the top, having dedicated CEOs who understand that ecology and economy no longer require a trade-off will boost a company's green endeavors. CEOs will increasingly be confronted with an increasing demand for sustainability from many stakeholders and they will be expected to have the answers to those issues at hand. The staff at all levels needs to be encouraged to take on leadership roles in the sustainability process. Strategic decisions must be supported by the entire organization. Convincing employees to apply 'greener' processes, which save resources and help the environment, should be on top of the hotel executives' agenda.

Raising the awareness of the staff is the first step. As has been pointed out in previous chapters, 'greening' does not always involve technology or capital investment. Small steps lead to greater efficiency, resource efficiency and financial savings. Being 'green' is a mind-set. And positive outcomes will happen when mind-sets evolve. So much attention is focused on the plight of our planet by the media that a momentum for change is developing in society; hotel executives are advised to follow this movement.

Once inspiring leadership has captured enthusiasm, environmental training procedures need to be installed. Only regular ongoing training sessions ensure that 'greener' processes become a matter of course. A 'green team' or a manager responsible for sustainability issues should look at operational areas that can be improved. Departmental heads should be made responsible for the implementation of improved processes and staff feedback should be encouraged. An assessment of environmental attitudes could become part of the recruitment process in human resource departments. Employees who are sensitive toward environmental issues are more willing to apply new environmental standards.

Industry analysts point out that employees are often more satisfied working for an employer that has concern for the environment. Staff environmental initiatives are good for company morale; staff turnover and, consequently, guest satisfaction are both positively influenced. Staff that are eager to act on environmental issues increase the likelihood of greater efficiency and greater financial returns.

Technologies and initiatives

Before actually thinking about the promotion of their efforts in sustainability, hotel companies must make sure that the green technologies and initiatives they wish to install keep their promise. The alternative is to be accused of greenwashing, thus damaging their valuable brand image. Many new technologies require high capital investments and their true cost/benefits are sometimes not sufficiently researched.

Know your customers

Hospitality operations are not always well equipped to attract environmentally sensitive consumers. Hotel companies would be well advised to gain feedback from guests on their behavior concerning environmental initiatives. At the very least, such enquiries sensitize customers to responsible marketing activities and 'green' branding. Although hotel sustainability might never become a unique selling proposition, it adds extra value in some sectors. A similar approach influences the guests' choice of holiday decisions.

Tourists are more sophisticated than ever before, sustainable holiday destinations are in vogue.

However, society is not ready for a bulldozer approach to sustainability, as environmental concern is the right of the individual. While fulfilling the expectations of guests is paramount in the job of all hospitality professionals, comfort and satisfaction can never be sacrificed. Fortunately, environmental concern is no longer a marginal activity, and care must be taken to ensure that guests become partners in environmental policy making. The role of hoteliers as educators should not be underestimated, and once hotels have clarity about their customers' views, the management can then start to satisfy their curiosity in what the establishment is doing in this domain.

Centralized actions

With the extensive organizational resources hotel chains have at their disposal, they have the power to bring about change on a large scale. Strong franchise systems and tight control systems ensure success. If individual units in hotel chains act independently on environmental issues, without special focus, short-term financial returns might be achieved but chain-branding opportunities will be lost. Actions must be centralized and consistent from unit to unit in order to create internal and external awareness. Moreover, a centralized approach reduces bureaucracy and repetition. Finally, centralization of actions facilitates strategic adjustments once the program is running.

CHAPTER QUESTIONS

1. What are the advantages in setting up an Environmental Management System within a hospitality property?

2. What are the challenges in setting up an Environmental Management System within a hospitality property?

3. How can you involve the employees in working with an Environmental Management System?

READING LIST

Accor Environnemental Report. <http://www.accor.com/gb/upload/pdf/doc_ref_2002/part8.pdf>

Eco-Management and Audit Scheme, 2009. Guidance documents. European Commission Environment DG, Brussels. Available at http://www.ec.europa.eu/environment/emas/documents/guidance_en.htm

Fairmont Hotels & Resorts Environmental Policy. <http://www.fairmont.com/EN_FA/AboutFairmont/environment/EnvironmentalPolicy/>

Hilton Environmental Programme. <http://www.hiltonwecare.com/>

InterContinental Hotel Group Corporate Social Responsibility Report. <http://www.ihgplc.com/index.asp?pageid=8>

International Standard Organization, 2009. ISO and the Environment. International Standard Organization, Geneva. Available at http://www.iso.org/iso/iso_catalogue/management_standards/iso_9000_iso_14000/iso_and_the_environment.htm

Marriott Social Responsibility Report. <http://www.marriott.com/Images/Text%20Images/US/MarriottSocialResponsibilityandCommunityEngagement.pdf>

Starkey, R., 1999. The standardization of environmental management systems: ISO 14001, ISO 14004 and EMAS. In: Welford, R. (Ed.), Corporate Environmental Management. Earthscan Publications Ltd, London, pp. 61–89.

Starwood Hotels & Resorts Worldwide Environmental Sustainability Policy. <http://www.starwoodhotels.com/corporate/company_values_env.html>

CHAPTER 13

Financing Schemes and Funds According to Sustainable Principles

Study Objectives

- To define the concept of green financing
- To understand the financing instrument and the benefits of green funds
- To provide a general overview of green financing examples
- To identify and discuss the critical assumptions related to large-scale sustainable development initiatives

GREEN FINANCING: INTRODUCTION

Despite the common belief that a high investment is required for the creation of sustainable buildings and facilities, it has been shown that by employing an integrated, holistic building-design strategy early in the planning process, the sustainability of the building structure is maximized without a considerable increase in costs. Sometimes a net reduction in the initial cost of a sustainable building can be achieved (Rincones, 2000), while in some cases where the capital cost is higher, the investment typically pays off during the first few years of operation. In addition, when applying principles of sustainable construction, low operating costs can lead to savings throughout the building's life cycle.

FINANCING INSTRUMENTS

Around the world, financing schemes have been created specifically for the promotion of more sustainable building practices.

The sustainable financing instruments available include 'green financing' and 'green investment' schemes initiated by governments to attract funding at reduced interest rates. Banks operating green investment funds sometimes offer loans even below the market interest rates. These investment funds are designated for projects that respect the principles of sustainable development or those facilities with environmentally friendly systems (improving energy efficiency, incorporation of renewable energy). Typically, at least 70% of the capital in a green fund must be committed to green projects. The benefits are typically threefold:

1. The company obtains a relatively cheap loan.
2. Private investors can invest their money at attractive rates.
3. The environment benefits in the long run.

Furthermore, there is a growing pool of green investment funds that invest in companies committed to ethical practices and also operating in cooperation with local communities.

SOME NATIONAL FINANCING EXAMPLES

Most industrialized countries have developed special financing schemes to encourage the development of structures compatible with the local natural environment and society at home and in developing countries.

Europe

The Netherlands and Denmark have many green investment funds and tax deduction schemes connected to environmental initiatives. The Gaia Trust of Denmark is a charitable foundation that supports the development of sustainable settlements across the globe and its eco-village called the Global Eco-village Network. This organization, in short GEN (http://gen.ecovillage.org/), has been set up to meet the needs of ecological settlements. Eco-villages are urban or rural communities where members strive to develop a low-impact way of life in society. To achieve this, they integrate various aspects of ecological design, ecological building, green production, alternative energy and community-building practices.

Eco-villages can now be found across the globe:

- GEN Oceania and Asia (http://genoa.ecovillage.org/)
- Ecovillage Network of the Americas (ENA) (http://ena.ecovillage.org/)

- EN Europe (http://www.gen-europe.org/)
- EN South East Asia (http://gen.ecovillage.org/regions/index.html)

In Germany, green funding is still relatively young. The main focus is on renewable energies and the financing of wind and solar energy. However, there are various projects based on cooperation between the federal states and regional government or city councils.

The federal state of Baden-Württemberg in cooperation with the city of Freiburg have pioneered Plusenergyhouses (houses producing more energy than is needed by the inhabitants of the house) and developed the first German solar real estate investment fund (http://www.freiburgersolarfonds.de). With the capital of this fond, the Solarsiedlung GmbH builds Plusenergyhouses in Freiburg (http://www.solarsiedlung.de).

The city of Freiburg has developed the so-called sustainable district of Freiburg-Vauban (http://www.forum-vauban.de). Old army barracks have been converted into new housing with the most modern sustainable technologies. The Hotel Victoria in the city is the first zero-emissions hotel in Germany (http://www.hotel-victoria.de).

In France also, all the major banks offer their customers similar investment possibilities. The Crédit Mutuel Bank offers a selection of green investment opportunities with its "Sérenité" unit trust and the Banque Populaire du Haut Rhin offers cheap loans in its PREVair initiative for companies investing in environmentally friendly projects.

North America

In the United States there exists a wide range of publications and tools related to green development financing, which are available online at the US Environmental Protection Agency site: http://www.epa.gov/greenbuilding/tools/funding.htm.

SUSTAINABLE FUNDING GUIDELINES

There is no strict or universally accepted definition on what makes a green or sustainable investment fund. However, green funds can be characterized as mutual funds that invest in socially and environmentally responsible companies.

We can discern five categories of sustainable or green funds, where each category might concern tourism projects:

1. Environmental leaders: companies whose core products are environmentally friendly.

2. Environmental pioneers: small innovative companies that are developing environmentally and socially friendly products.

3. Ethical-minded companies: companies that have a strong ethical policy.

4. Environmental technology companies: companies that are involved in sewage and rubbish disposal or wind energy.

5. Sustainable companies: companies that incorporate the principles of sustainability at all stages of the business cycle.

Many banks offer sustainable investment funds to investors and 'green' bonds to private individuals who have the desire to save money in an environmentally friendly manner. Unfortunately, some of the banks offering green funds do not make information freely available on why these funds are called 'green' and on which principles of sustainability they rely.

SUSTAINABLE DEVELOPMENT INITIATIVES: ASSUMPTIONS AND FACTS

Buildings and other construction developments are capital-intensive undertakings that require the active cooperation of all actors in financial markets. Therefore, the issue of project financing is among the most important aspects of facility development.

The authors of Financing Change have identified six assumptions that are critical for large-scale sustainable development initiatives. These include (Schmidheiny, Zorraquin and WBCSD, 1996):

1. Eco-efficiency favors long term profitability.

2. By not internalizing environmental costs, the benefits of eco-efficiency are not easily identifiable.

3. Most tax systems favor labor productivity over resource efficiency.

4. Accounting systems do not adequately address environmental issues.

5. Sustainable development deals with the future which is generally ignored by financial markets.

6. Sustainable development is often associated with high-risk investments, especially in developing countries.

In addition, a widespread (and equally misplaced) belief that environmental measures are prohibitively expensive prevails among the industry representatives, and is perhaps the greatest barrier preventing hospitality operators from promoting 'greener' establishments.

In many instances, the division of facility ownership, operation and management among different stakeholders is an additional barrier to the implementation of more environmentally responsible business practices. When a tourism operator/manager contracts a building on a fixed monthly rent, regardless of the water and energy quantities consumed, the building owner may not be willing to invest in additional energy and/or water-saving measures. A mutual and close cooperation of all stakeholders involved in finding a solution beneficial to all partners is ultimately required.

While the necessary modifications in technology, management and behavior may require substantial investments, numerous credible showcase examples indicate that investments in greater sustainability are profitable in the long run.

FINANCING SCHEME

Funding for specific 'end of pipe' measures to reduce water and airborne pollution and cut the use of non-renewable energy resources is widely available. Legislation to curb pollution has increased in recent years and companies are obliged to modify their activities. However, legislation compelling individuals and companies to use alternative energy resources are few and far between. Some countries in Europe have introduced eco-taxes to penalize

CASE STUDY 13.1: Sustainable Investment Scheme

Jupiter International Group PLC is among the institutions offering green financing to companies all over the world. The Jupiter Green Investment Trust PLC's portfolio has a bias toward small- and medium-sized companies. It performs within the framework of Jupiter Green, which includes three distinct funding schemes (Jupiter, 2004): Jupiter Ecology Fund, Jupiter Environmental Opportunities Fund and Jupiter Global Green Investment Trust.

The Group invests in products and services that provide solutions to environmental and social problems. It invests in companies whose activities lead to the improvement of air quality, water availability and quality, the creation of better waste-management schemes, more sustainable transport and more healthy lifestyles as well as in companies that help other actors on the market comply with environment-related regulations.

The second group of projects financed by Jupiter Green include companies working to reduce the environmental impacts of their operations, by incorporating environmental management systems. These projects work towards; resource-use efficiency, decreasing the impacts from company-related transportation, purchasing from sustainable sources and protecting local and global diversity. Jupiter Green also favors companies that design their products to minimize environmental life-cycle impacts.

The third major target group are companies that work to improve the social impacts of their operations. Companies having fair employment practices, good health and safety conditions and requiring their suppliers to respect the same conditions are preferred. Jupiter Green favors companies with active policies designed to eliminate and prevent bribery and corruption within their operations. Only companies that respect national legislation, the UN Declaration of Human Rights and the International Labour Organisation receive financial help. In addition, fostering good relationships with the local community are also encouraged.

Source: Jupiter Assest Management, www.jupiteronline.co.uk

heavy users of fossil fuels, and pressure from lobby groups is being put on the US government to bring in legislation as well.

Many subsidies exist in Germany and France to encourage companies to use alternative forms of energy. In Germany, these grants and tax reductions come mainly from regional governments and in France from the government funded Agence de l'Environnement et de la Maitrise de l'Energie. Countries throughout the European Union can also benefit from the LIFE-Programme for financing. LIFE is a EU financial instrument supporting environmental and nature conservation projects. Since 1992, LIFE has co-financed some 2,750 projects, contributing approximately €1.35 billion to the protection of the environment. (LIFE, 2009). The Competitiveness and Innovation Framework Programme (CIP) of the EU is particularly interesting for the hospitality industry. The Competitiveness and Innovation Framework Programme (CIP) aims to encourage the competitiveness of European enterprises. With small and medium-sized enterprises (SMEs) as its main target, the programme supports innovation activities (including eco-innovation), provide better access to finance and deliver business support services. The programme has for a particular objective to promote the increased use of renewable energies and energy efficiency. Until 2013, pilot eco-innovation projects may be eligible for funding under the Entrepreneurship and Innovation Programme (EIP), a sub-programme of the Competitiveness and Innovation Framework Programme (CIP). The EIP sub-programme ensures a better access to finance for SMEs through venture capital investment and loan guarantee instruments. It also supports promotion of entrepreneurship and innovation in the world of eco-innovation. The funding priorities are buildings, food & drink, greening business, and smart purchasing. €28 million worth of funding will be available covering up to 60% of the eligible costs (EIP).

CHAPTER QUESTIONS

1. Explain why a hospitality business should look for green financing or green funding when undertaking a renovation project?

2. When investing, what sort of green investment schemes exist and what are the advantages of investing in such schemes?

READING LIST

Bouma, J.J., Jeucken, M., Klinkers, L. Deloitte & Touche, 2001. Sustainable Banking: The Greening of Finance. Greenleaf Publishing, Sheffield, UK.

Holliday, C.O., Schmidheiny, S., Watts, P. World Business Council for Sustainable Development, 2002. Walking the Talk: The Business Case for Sustainable Development. Greenleaf Publishing, Sheffield, UK.

Institute for Applied Ecology (Öko-Institut e.V.). <http://www.oeko.de/home/dok/546.php>

Jupiter's Investment Approach. <http://www.jupiterinternational.com/Professional+Investors/About_Us/Investment_Approach/>

Life. <http://ec.europa.eu/environment/life/>

Rincones, D., 2000. Green Building Resource Guide. US Environmental Protection Agency Region 5, Chicago, IL.

Schmidheiny, S., Zorraquin, F.J.L. World Business Council for Sustainable Development, 1998. Financing Change. MIT Press, Cambridge, MA.

US Environmental Protection Agency Funding Opportunities. <http://www.epa.gov/greenbuilding/tools/funding.htm>

Conclusion

In the past few years, some sectors of the hospitality industry have made progress toward managing operations in a sustainable manner. With initiatives such as the implementation of energy efficient practices, employee training and education programs, waste and water management and the development of eco-design building, the greening of the industry is becoming a reality. Yet, the status quo within the industry regarding sustainable development is still far from optimal. It is imperative for hoteliers to move beyond current governmental regulations in order to achieve sustainability as defined by the World Business Council on Sustainable Development.

Competition in the hospitality sector is fierce amid the growing and constantly changing business and leisure market. In addition, the hotel sector has experienced a steep increase in energy and water costs coupled with raised consumer expectations regarding how we treat the natural environment and society at large. Due to the immensity of this industry, the resulting impacts are not to be underestimated, both positively in terms of economic growth and, unfortunately, negatively as witnessed by resource depletion, loss of biodiversity and the dislocation of local people in some areas of hospitality development.

Counteracting these negative impacts requires dedication from owners, management and employees with continuous training on sustainability, open discussion with consumers, investment in clean technologies and a long-term business partnership outlook that embraces all stakeholders.

The world of hospitality must reflect on its role in terms of social and environmental responsibility. While some companies tend to be in reactive mode when it comes to change, i.e following best practices, some have been taking a lead in terms of social and ethical accounting and environmental auditing and reporting. Private and governmental organizations have proposed processes for standardization and accreditation to companies wishing to provide their stakeholders with an integrated approach to social, environmental and ethical benchmarking.

Hospitality professionals and civil society in both on- and offline communities must continue to forge a new sustainable future together through a more responsible business behavior.

Glossary of Sustainable Development for Hotels and Restaurants

Accreditation A procedure to establish if a tourism business meets certain standards of management and operation.

AECB The Association for Environment Conscious Building promotes environmentally responsible practices within building.

Agenda 21 Program of action adopted by the 1992 United Nations Conference on Environment and Development.

Assets Something of value that will provide future benefit or utility, can be used to generate revenue. Usually owned, so simply described as 'things we own'.

Auditing A process to measure and verify the practices of a business.

Benchmarking Process of comparing performance and activities among similar organizations either against an agreed standard or against those that are recognized as being among the best.

Benchmarks Points of reference or comparison, which may include standards, critical success factors, indicators, metrics.

Best Practice Operational standards considered the most effective and efficient means of achieving desired outcomes.

Biodiversity Shorthand for biological diversity: the variability among living organisms. It includes diversity within species, between species and of ecosystems.

Brundtland Report The report of the World Commission on Environment and Development (WCED), entitled "Our Common Future" published in 1987. The report established the internationally accepted definition of sustainability.

Capital Expenditure The cost of long-term assets, such as computer equipment, vehicles and premises. These assets are bought to use over several years and not to resell.

Carbon dioxide (CO_2) A greenhouse gas produced through respiration and the decomposition of organic substances. Combustion of fossil fuels is primarily responsible for increased atmospheric concentrations of this gas.

171

Carbon Footprint A representation of the effect human activities have on the climate in terms of the total amount of greenhouse gases produced (measured in units of carbon dioxide).

Carbon Offsetting The counter balancing of carbon emissions through the purchase of a carbon credit to help fund projects that reduce/offset overall greenhouse gas emissions.

Cause-Related Marketing Used where a company allies itself with a specific cause, and contributes money, time or expertise to an organization or event for that cause in return for the right to make publicity or commercial value from that involvement.

CFLs Compact fluorescent lights.

Climate Change Change in regional or global temperature and weather patterns.

Code of Ethics/Conduct/Practice Recommended practices based on a system of self-regulation intended to promote environmentally and/or socioculturally sustainable behavior.

Composting Biological process used to treat organic waste (green waste, fermentable fraction of municipal waste, sludge from urban treatment plants, etc.), by degrading them in an accelerated manner.

Conservation Can be broadly interpreted as action taken to protect and preserve the natural world from harmful features of tourism, including pollution and overexploitation of resources.

CSR Corporate Social Responsibility is a concept by which companies integrate the interests and needs of customers, employees, suppliers, shareholders, communities and the planet into corporate strategies.

Degradation Any decline in the quality of natural or cultural resources, or the viability of ecosystems, that is caused directly or indirectly by humans.

DFD Design for Disassembly ensure that when products are obsolete, they can easily and economically be taken apart, components reused or repaired.

Dow Jones Sustainability Index The Dow Jones Sustainability Index is one of the first global indexes watching the financial performance of leading companies with an emphasis on sustainability in economic, social and environmental capacities.

Eco-Design Also referred to as Sustainable Design, Environmental Design, Environmentally Sustainable Design or Environmentally-Conscious Design. It is the philosophy of designing objects or buildings according to the principles of economic, social, and environmental sustainability.

Eco-Label Information (typically provided on a label attached to a product) informing a potential consumer of a product's characteristics, or of the production or processing method(s) used in its production.

Ecologically Sustainable Using, conserving and enhancing the community's resources so that ecological development is maintained, and the total quality of life can be sustained now and in the future.

Ecosystem A dynamic system of plant, animal, fungal and microorganism communities, and the associated non-living physical and chemical factors.

Ecotax Short for ecological taxation which is a policy introducing taxes intended to promote ecologically sustainable activities.

Ecotourism Ecologically sustainable tourism with a primary focus on experiencing natural areas that foster environmental and cultural understanding, appreciation and conservation.

EMAS Eco-Management and Audit Scheme.

Energy Conservation Positive initiatives to reduce the consumption of energy to the minimum level required.

Environment The ecosystem in which an organism or a species lives, including both the physical environment and the other organisms with which it comes in contact.

Environmental Auditing Inspection of a tourism organization to assess the environmental impact of its activities.

Environmental Impact The effects that a community has on the environment as a consequence of its activities.

Environmental Impact Assessment A study undertaken to assess the effect of an action upon a specific environment or the social or cultural integrity of a community.

Environmental Management System (EMS) System that a tourism organization can use to implement its environmental policy and achieve associated objectives to control environmental impacts significant of its activities and to respect regulatory requirements.

Environmental Stewardship Long-term management aimed at preserving and enhancing the quality of an environment.

FLO International The Fairtrade Labelling Organizations International is an umbrella organization whose mission is to set the Fairtrade Standards, support, inspect and certify disadvantaged producers and harmonize the Fairtrade message.

Food Miles A calculation of the distance and mode of transport foodstuffs have traveled throughout the complete production process and until they reach the consumer.

Footprint (Ecological) A measure of the hectares of biologically productive area required to support a human population of given size.

GDP The Gross Domestic Product is a measure of the total value of goods and services produced by the domestic economy during a given period, usually 1 year.

Global Reporting Initiative (GRI) A private initiative offering sustainability reporting guidelines that take into account environmental, social and economic performance.

Globalization Generally defined as the network of connections of organizations and peoples are across national, geographic and cultural borders and boundaries. These global networks are creating a shrinking world where local differences and national boundaries are being subsumed into global identities. Within the field of tourism, globalization is also viewed in terms of the revolutions in telecommunications, finance and transport that are key factors currently influencing the nature and pace of growth of tourism in developing nations.

Green Globe/Green Globe 21 Green Globe 21 is the worldwide benchmarking and certification program which facilitates sustainable travel and tourism for consumers, companies and communities. It is based on Agenda 21 and principles for Sustainable Development endorsed by 182 governments at the United Nations Rio de Janeiro Earth Summit in 1992.

Greenhouse Gas A gas such as carbon dioxide or methane that reflects infrared radiation emitted by the earth, thereby helping to retain heat in the atmosphere.

Green Marketing Integrating business practices and products that are friendly to the environment while also meeting the needs of the consumers.

Greenwash The unjustified appropriation of environmental virtue by a company, an industry, a government, a politician or even a non-government organization to create a pro-environmental image, sell a product or a policy.

Heritage Things of value that are inherited which people want to keep. Heritage can be natural, cultural, tangible, intangible, personal or collective. Natural heritage is often conserved in places such as reserves and national parks. Cultural heritage practices are often conserved through ongoing traditions and practices.

Hospitality Industry Industry made up of businesses that provide accommodation, provide food and beverages, provide entertainment.

HOTREC The European Hotel and Restaurant Association is the spokesperson of hotels, restaurants and cafés at European institutional level.

HVAC Heating, ventilation and air conditioning.

ICC The International Chamber of Commerce created a Business Charter for Sustainable Development comprising 16 principles for environmental management.

IFOAM The International Federation of Organic Agriculture Movements is the worldwide umbrella organization for the organic agriculture movement.

IH&RA   The International Hotel and Restaurant Association.

Impacts   Effects, which may be either positive or negative, felt as a result of tourism-associated activity. Tourists have at least three kinds of impacts on a destination: economic, sociocultural and environmental. Tourism also has effects on tourists, in terms of possible attitude and behavior changes.

Indicator   A summary measure that provides information on the state of, or change in, a system.

ISO   International Organization for Standardization.

kWh   Kilowatt-hour is a unit of energy equivalent to one kilowatt of power expended for one hour of time.

LED   Light-Emitting Diode.

LEED   The Leadership in Energy and Environmental Design is a green building rating and certification program.

Life cycle   The particular pattern through which a destination evolves.

Life Cycle Assessment (LCA)   LCA is the investigation and valuation of the environmental, economic and social impacts of a product or service. A product's life cycle starts when the raw materials are extracted from the earth through to processing, transport, use, reuse, recycling or disposal. For each of these stages, the impact is measured in terms of the resources used and environmental impacts caused.

Lifestyle   A person's pattern of living as expressed in his or her activities, interests and opinions.

LOHAS   Lifestyles of Health and Sustainability is a demographic defining a particular market segment related to sustainable living.

LOVOS   Lifestyle of Voluntary Simplicity is a socio-demographic segment oriented to health and sustainability particularly critical of consumption and consumerism.

Mass Tourism   Traditional, large-scale tourism commonly, but loosely used to refer to popular forms of leisure tourism pioneered in southern Europe, the Caribbean and North America in the 1960s and 1970s.

Monitoring   The ongoing review and assessment of the natural or cultural integrity of a place in order to detect changes in its condition with reference to a baseline condition.

NGO   Non-governmental organization refers to a non-profit making, voluntary, service-oriented or development-oriented organization, either for the benefit of members or of other members of the population.

Photovoltaic (Solar) Cell   Generally speaking, a device incorporating a semiconductor that generates electricity when exposed to (sun) light. The technology may be further subdivided into crystalline, multi-crystalline, thin-film and concentrator variants.

Pollution   Harmful effects on the environment as a by-product of tourism activity. Types include air, noise, water and aesthetic.

Public Policy   Is whatever governments choose to do or not to do (Thomas Dye, 1992: 2). Such a definition covers government action, inaction, decisions and non-decisions as it implies a very deliberate choice between alternatives (see Hall and Jenkins, 1995).

Recycling   The process by which discarded materials are collected, sorted, processed and converted into raw materials which are then used in the production of new products.

Renewable Energy   Energy sources that are practically inexhaustible. For example, solar, hydro and wind energy.

Renewable Resource   A resource that is capable of being replenished through natural processes or its own reproduction, generally within a time-span that does not exceed a few decades.

Responsible Tourism   Type of tourism which is practiced by tourists who make responsible choices when choosing their holidays. These choices reflect responsible attitudes to the limiting of the extent of the sociological and environmental impacts their holiday may cause.

SME(s)   Small and medium-sized enterprises.

Social   Relating to human society and interaction between its members.

Social Impacts Assessment (SIA)   A methodology to review the social effects of effects of a public or private policy, program or infrastructure project on surrounding populations.

Soil Association   The Soil Association is a charity which promotes and develops sustainable approaches to food, farming and other products.

Stakeholder   Any person, group or organization with an interest in, or who may be affected by, the activities of another organization.

Sustainable   Something which can be kept in the same or a better condition for the future.

Sustainable Development   Development carried out in such a way as to meet the needs of the present without compromising the ability of future generations to meet their needs.

Sustainable Tourism   Tourism that can be sustained over the long term because it results in a net benefit for the social, economic, natural and cultural environments of the area in which it takes place.

Sustainability   Sustainability is effectively the goal of sustainable development. It is the ideal end state which we must aspire.

Tourist   Anyone who spends at least one night away from home, no matter what the purpose is.

Triple Bottom Line   An expanded baseline for measuring performance, adding social and environmental dimensions to the traditional monetary benchmark.

UNCED   The United Nations Conference on Environment and Development promotes global cooperation between developing and industrialized countries in planning and managing environmentally responsible development.

UNEP   The United Nations Environment Programme coordinates United Nations environmental activities.

UNWTO   The United Nations World Tourism Organization is a United Nations agency dealing with questions relating to tourism.

VISIT   The Voluntary Initiatives for Sustainability in Tourism promotes and supports sustainable tourism development through the representation, promotion and mutual cooperation of international, national and regional certification schemes.

WBCSD   The World Business Council on Sustainable Development is a global association of some 200 international companies dealing exclusively with business and sustainable development.

Willingness-to-Pay   The amount an individual is willing to pay to acquire some good or service. This amount can be elicited from the individual's stated or revealed preferences.

World Economic Forum   The WEF is an independent economic organization best known for its annual meeting in Davos, Switzerland which brings together top business leaders, international political leaders, selected intellectuals and journalists to discuss the most pressing issues facing the world.

World Social Forum   The WSF is an annual meeting held by members of the anti-globalization movement.

Worldwatch Institute   A globally-focused environmental research organization based in Washington, D.C.

WRAP   Waste & Resources Action Programme is a not-for-Profit UK company helping individuals, businesses and local authorities to reduce waste, encourage recycling and help tackle climate change.

WWF   The World Wide Fund For Nature aims to conserve nature and ecological processes by preserving biodiversity, ensuring sustainable use of natural resources and promoting the reduction of pollution and wasteful use of resources and energy.

(*Sources*: Organization for Economic Co-Operation and Development (OECD), International Institute for Sustainable Development (IISD)).

Index